JOSÉ MARTÍ

José Martí: An Introduction

Oscar Montero

First published 2004 by PALGRAVE MACMILLAN™
175 Fifth Avenue, New York, N.Y. 10010 and
Houndmills, Basingstoke, Hampshire, England RG21 6XS.
Companies and representatives throughout the world.

PALGRAVE MACMILLAN is the global academic imprint of the Palgrave Macmillan division of St. Martin's Press, LLC and of Palgrave Macmillan Ltd. Macmillan® is a registered trademark in the United States, United Kingdom and other countries. Palgrave is a registered trademark in the European Union and other countries.

Brief excerpts from *A Coney Island of the Mind,* copyright © 1958 by Lawrence Ferlinghetti. Reprinted by permission of New Directions Publishing Corp.

ISBN 1-4039-6286-3 hardback
ISBN 1-4039-6287-1 paperback

Library of Congress Cataloging-in-Publication Data

Montero, Oscar, 1947-
    José Martí : an introduction / Oscar Montero.
        p. cm.
    Includes bibliographical references and index
    ISBN 1-4039-6286-3 (alk. Paper) – ISBN 1-4039-6287-1 (pbk. : alk. paper)
    Martí, José, 1853-1895—Exile—New York (N.Y.) 2. Martí, José, 1853-1895—Views on the United States. 3. United States—Civilization—19th century 4. United States—History—1865-1898 I. Title

F1783.M38M645 2003
972.91'05'092–dc22   2003058139

A catalogue record for this book is available from the British Library.

Design by Kolam Information Services Pvt. Ltd, Pondicherry, India.

First edition: April 2004
10 9 8 7 6 5 4 3 2 1

Printed in the United States of America.

A mi madre Lilia Díaz Valdés

Contents

Acknowledgements

There are forms of collaboration that are not credited in the list of works cited. A debt is owed not just to those whose criticism and scholarship helped me to write this book but to others who offered suggestions, opened spaces in which to air out questions and gave their enthusiasm and support. It is satisfying to look back on the work nearly completed, edit the memory of the rough patches and acknowledge the help of others.

Antonio Vera-León read the manuscript and offered sharp comments, which I used during revisions, especially in the prologue. His intelligence, warmth and generosity are much appreciated. I thank my friends Licia Fiol-Matta and José Quiroga, editors of this series, for their interest in my work on Martí, long before it took its present form. During the years I worked on this book, I was invited to lecture, participate in panels and give courses on Martí. I thank the friends and colleagues who provided these opportunities to present my work. On many occasions, my conversations with José Gomariz helped me to think of new ways to tackle one problem or another.

Colleagues, friends and family gave me or sent me books, articles and clippings, which were often useful and always a pleasure to receive. One such gift was a book that does not appear in the works cited, although I consulted it often, the *Atlas histórico biográfico José Martí* (historical, biographical José Martí atlas), given to me by Martí scholars Ibrahim Hidalgo and Pedro Pablo Rodríguez. Nuria Gregori gave me a copy of her facsimilar edition of Martí's diary, which helped me not only to unravel some of its riddles but also to have a sense of its physical reality, frayed pages crisscrossed with Martí's writing, his erasures and corrections.

When I needed the complete works of Martí, my cousin Raimundo Montero found me a set in Havana. I doubt I could have completed this book without those volumes on hand in my office here in New York. My aunt in Cuba, Yara Díaz, sent me numerous articles and photographs; she, my late aunt Ana Díaz, and my mother Lilia, to whom I dedicate this book, have kept alive for me a connection to Cuban history and culture that is also part of the story of our family.

In my courses at Lehman College and The Graduate Center, City University of New York, the questions and suggestions of students helped me to reconsider many aspects of this book. I was grateful for their patience with my enthusiasm for Martí and happy when they sometimes shared it. Parts of chapters 2 and 3 were published in the electronic journal *Ciberletras*, whose editors Cristina Guiñazú and Susana

Haydu I thank. Ella Pearce, my editor at Palgrave, offered her enthusiasm and support from the time I first proposed this book. I thank her and production editor Sonia Wilson for overseeing the copyediting and guiding the book through the process of publication.

I am grateful for my family, for their love and support, even when great distances and insurmountable barriers have separated us. I thank Johnny Loflin, my partner of many years, for our love, for always being there and for knowing when not to be.

Oscar Montero
New York, N. Y.
December 3, 2003

Prologue

From Coney Island to Dos Ríos*

In the din of the city, who pauses before a statue? Who bothers to read
what is carved in stone? In New York City, no one says "the Avenue of
the Americas" to refer to what has always been Sixth Avenue. Walking
uptown on this avenue, the urban stroller comes to one of the grand
entrances at the southern boundary of Central Park. The entrance is
guarded by the equestrian statues of three great Latin American heroes:
Simón Bolívar, José de San Martín and José Martí. I went there on a
frigid afternoon in late January to see if someone had placed flowers to
honor the day of Martí's birthday, the 28th. It turns out there were two
funeral wreaths, one of them with dozens of white rosebuds, placed
there by the Cuban Cultural Center of New York. This book, a reading
of Martí, an introduction to "the man and his works," begins at this
spot. For me it has always been a place that is both familiar and alienating. It is familiar because the image of Martí brings back memories of
my Cuban childhood. It is alienating because there is something
anachronistic and unsettling about a granite monolith topped by a rearing horse and its heroic rider in the heart of Manhattan, the place where
I live.

The statue at the southern edge of Central Park, at Artists' Gate, was
placed there in 1965, at the height of the Cold War. In its strained
grandeur, it pays homage to a myth: a poet turned revolutionary, a man
who found virtue in sacrifice and heroism in death. It commemorates
action and movement with the massive stillness of bronze and stone—a

---

*Unless otherwise noted, all references to Martí's works are from *Obras comple-
tas* [complete works] Havana: Editorial de Ciencias Sociales, 1975, and are given
parenthetically, by volume and page number. Unless otherwise noted, all translations are mine.

rearing horse in a doomed charge. The statue has nothing else to say, and even its compact message is lost on most of the thousands of people who walk by it every day. If the statue celebrates heroic action, then Martí's words, the other side of the old equation, are another story. Rather, they are a series of possible stories, stories that have demanded reading and interpretation from generations of readers.

José Martí was born in Havana, January 28, 1853. He died in a Cuban battlefield on May 19, 1895. He was both a nineteenth-century hero and a man with a fearful vision of the century to come. It was a vision crafted for the people Martí called *los latinos, la gente latina*, Latin people. By "*latinos*" Martí meant people from Latin America, wherever they might be: Mexico, New York, Tampa or Key West. One may certainly argue that "latino" and "Latin people" in the work of Martí are far removed from contemporary debates around the notion of "Latino-America," which center on, or rather circle, approach and negotiate the question of national identity and its relationship to our many diasporas. It would be impossible in these pages to do justice to the complexity of the topic and the vast bibliography it has produced.

Moreover, it would be simplistic to suggest that Martí's own ideas about "Latinity" and identity somehow prefigure our own contemporary debates. However, in Martí's use of "*los latinos*" there is a sense of identity that is resonant today; that is, identity as the sharing of values, cultural and even spiritual values, and the sharing of common purposes beyond the geographic and political limitations imposed by discrete identities. In this sense, Martí's use of "latino" does prefigure its contemporary uses in suggestive ways. It is my hope that some of those suggestions and their implications today become evident in the pages that follow. Among other topics, the question of "identity" is discussed in chapters five and six.

Writing about Martí in English has been for me a rather uneasy compromise between translation and gloss, between commentary and interpretation. To borrow the title of an article by Antonio Vera-León, in this "garden of forking tongues," an echo of Borges's short story, I have perhaps tried to appease the devils of my own bilingual anxieties through the work of interpreting Martí in English.

In *Cuba on my Mind*, contemporary critic Román de la Campa writes of his experience of "doubleness" as an exile. In a brief but significant aside, de la Campa argues that for Martí, "[b]eing Cuban ultimately went beyond the national" (119). The statement might scandalize defenders of Martí's status as an inviolate national icon. However, it is certainly compatible with Martí's thinking about the politics of identity, which for Martí was as much art as politics, not the hard-line of a political agenda but the give-and-take of compromise, the craft of persuasion and the arts of representation.

In his brief comments on Martí, de la Campa writes of Martí's "commitment to traverse the incompatible spheres of pure aesthetics and committed politics" (119). These spheres may have become incompatible for us, but for Martí they were inexorably linked. The tension between art and politics or, in different terms, between the expressions of human subjectivity and the demands of a world of others, is central in Martí's writings. In a thorough study of Martí's reception in the twentieth century, originally written in German and translated into Spanish in 1995, Ottmar Ette argues that the question of art versus politics in Martí has been manipulated in readings and often misreadings determined by the complex cycles of Cuban and Latin American histories. To give but one example from Ette's "history of Martí's reception," in the 1930s and '40s the image of Martí was found "alongside political power, but also on the side of its adversaries, as well as on the side of those who kept a certain distance from politics" (128).

Ette concludes that "the division between a 'political' Martí and a 'literary' Martí continues to be a central problem in studies on the poet and revolutionary. There is still no organic understanding of the totality of Martí's works, one that would not subordinate unilaterally one aspect to the other" (408). My brief, selective comments on Martí and his works can hardly pretend to provide such an "organic understanding." In the limited space of these pages, I have tried to be mindful of the tradition so expertly reconstructed by Ette without presuming to account for all its ambiguities. In any case, there is no innocent return to Martí's text. Every reading brings along its own ideological baggage, sometimes all too evident, other times subtle yet no less corrosive. Nevertheless, I have tried to provide a context for these readings of Martí's selected texts and to suggest something of their potential and their contradictions, in ways that might be useful to a new reader looking for a few signposts in a rather overwhelming corpus.

Martí's sense of identity had its core in his own Cuba, Martí's heart, but it was quick to embrace Puerto Rico and the Dominican Republic, the respective origins of some of Martí's most loyal allies. It expanded to become an Antillean coalition and then came to include all of "our America." It was in fact a plea for human solidarity beyond borders, as urgent today as it was when it was uttered in a world that only wistful nostalgia could imagine as a simpler time. In the cautious language of today, we might say that there are unresolved issues with Martí's hopeful call for unity, especially around the questions of race and the role of women in the republic. In chapters two and three respectively, I discuss some of the questions raised by race and gender in Martí's works.

Critics have used many images to represent various aspects of Martí and his works. For example, it has often been said that the man, the myth and the text have fused in an inextricable bond, a metaphor that suggests an affective cohesion as irreversible as a chemical reaction. In an agricultural version of this metaphor, critic Angel Rama explains that Martí brings a poetic vision even to mundane commentaries, so that "analysis is always irrigated by the emotions" (168). Martí's text has been called a web, but it has also been likened to a vast quarry from which the critic must extract the diamond in the rough, a handsome if conventional mineral metaphor. A reader of Martí must confront this intricate symbolic pattern, crafted over the years by generations of readers. Critical metaphors can be useful in understanding Martí and his works. They can also become trite and restrictive. Images of Martí as prophet, saint, redeemer, apostle and even a celestial body abound, often in encomia that recycle a familiar rhetoric, which often glosses over Martí's words with cavalier insouciance.

The last thing Martí needs is another eulogy. Generations of politicos and keynote speakers have pounded that rhetoric into near nonsense. In "Martí and the Heroic Image," Oscar R. Martí synthesizes the changes in the cultural and political uses of Martí throughout the twentieth century. The many attempts to claim "the image of Martí" have often turned out to be "a race not for the discovery of an individual, but for the copyright of a myth" (329).

Many contemporary critics and scholars are carrying on work that is revealing new facets of Martí and his works. There have been laudable close readings of Martí's best-known works, notably "Nuestra América" (Our America) and "Mi raza" (My race). At the same time, it is useful to have a general understanding of Martí's ideas as a prelude to a closer reading, as it is possible to find justifications in the work of Martí for seemingly contradictory ideas. French scholar Paul Estrade has said that quoting has produced a "profusely mutilated Martí" (37). A more arduous but perhaps more helpful task is to give a sense of the way Martí embodied contradictions, adapting his position to circumstances, whether addressing a roomful of workers in a political speech or a close friend in a letter.

When the most admired and most familiar Martí is a carved monolith, it is difficult to confront a "Martí" whose persona is more fluid and more elusive. Not only because of its meaning but also by virtue of its context, a comment to a close friend in a letter has a different value from a statement made to a packed auditorium in New York City. The difference should be obvious, but many readings of Martí have taken the isolated quote as a true marker of "the man." In this reading, I have tried to give a sense of the context of Martí's words, so that others might get, if not the whole picture, certainly a valid outline, one that they may follow in their own subsequent readings.

Many of Martí's essays were published in Mexico, Caracas and Buenos Aires, and they show a keen awareness of the needs and circumstances of specific audiences. Other essays were first presented as speeches to various groups, often working people who gave their modest but essential support to the cause of Cuba. The style, the tone and the writer's stance obviously shift from one situation to another. This plurality of Martí the writer contrasts with the univocal rigidity of his image as a national icon. Readers of all stripes have not always come to terms with this seeming contradiction and have treated his texts as either polished literary masterpieces or political tracts. They were neither, and they were both. Many of the boundaries we take for granted, notably between "life" and "art," and between "art" and "politics," would have puzzled Martí. For him, the ways to navigate these areas were fluid and unpredictable, suited to the issues at hand not predetermined by neatly demarcated patterns.

Martí did not write for a "common reader," unchanged and steady from one context to another. He published hundreds of *crónicas* (chronicles), articles and essays in journals and newspapers scattered all over the Americas. In 1882, in New York City, he published a slim volume entitled *Ismaelillo* based on the love of a father for his son. It circulated among Martí's friends. It also revolutionized Spanish American poetry, ushering in what would later be called *modernismo*. Also in New York, in 1891 he published a small edition of his *Versos sencillos* (simple verses), a lyrical autobiography and today one of the best-known collections of verse ever written in the Spanish language. His radical *Versos libres* (free verses) and many other poems were published posthumously. The difficulty of editing these works, especially *Versos libres*, is evident in the thorough annotations by Martí scholar Ivan Schulman in the excellent Cátedra (Madrid) edition of the poems. In his final days, Martí left instructions on ways to arrange his work, putting special emphasis on his essays about the United States. The work of editing the thousands of pages he wrote began haltingly after his death. To this day it continues in earnest in Cuba's Centro de Estudios Martianos (Center for Martí Studies), founded in 1977.

In Martí's texts, whether speeches given to cigar workers or essays written for the Latin American press, there is often an urgent message.

There is of course the call for Cuba's independence from Spain, the core of all of Martí's efforts. At the same time, there are aspects of this message that are still resonant today. There is a call for commitment and compassion, praise for the life of the mind, a sustained warning against the traps of materialism and a stoic faith in the betterment of humankind. These are familiar topics, but Martí stated them with brilliant, enduring urgency. Often, in a paragraph bristling with sometimes over-burdened metaphors, one phrase stands out, capturing a thought or an idea with dazzling precision.

I have already said that the bibliography about Martí and his work is dauntingly vast. Indeed, in writing these pages I have relied on the work of many others, and have done my share of fretting over inclusions and inevitable oversights. The list of "Works Cited" is but a partial record of this debt. I decided to forgo all footnotes, for fear that they would overwhelm the text and subvert its aim as an introduction. Any work on Martí is a work of selection and omission, as if each new reader constructed his or her own book from a vast text uncontainable in a finite number of volumes. I hope my selections have been judicious. My goal is to give a sense of the range of Martí's most pertinent and most influential ideas, especially as they relate to the history and culture of the United States, a vast topic admirably covered in a founding work that I have often consulted. I am referring to Manuel Pedro González's *José Martí: Epic Chronicler of the United States in the Eighties*, published in 1953, the year of Martí's centennial, by the University of North Carolina, my alma mater.

It has often been said that Martí was an idealist, with an impossibly lofty conception of human destiny. The more I read him the more I see him as an unblinking realist, who nonetheless maintained an unshaken faith in humankind's potential to "feed the light and starve the beast": "Es indispensable alimentar la luz y achicar la bestia" (10:375). In the words of one of my students at Lehman College, a young actor named Noel Méndez, Martí's "ideas were not just a criticism of things as they were but a foreshadowing of things to come." I hope some aspects of Martí's lucid "foreshadowing" are evident in the pages that follow.

In Cuba, the image of Martí is ubiquitous, reproduced in thousands of busts, photographs, paintings and caricatures. His face is on Cuba's one peso bank note. The house in Havana where Martí was born 150 years ago has been visited by thousands of people. Standing on a street corner in New York City, I was startled to see Martí's prominent forehead and piercing eyes on the side of a passing bus, advertising a new rum! In Cuba and Latin America, the heroic Martí has a prominent place in the popular imagination, yet significant aspects of his legacy are not widely known. In the United States, outside of academia, his name is vaguely connected with Cuba, and now with this new brand of rum. I hope this small book is a reference point for what should be an ongoing debate, provoked by Martí and his works, a dialogue free of arid impasses, enlightened in the best sense of the word, a word already frayed in Martí's time but one whose power he wanted to rekindle. I am referring to a debate among Cubans, here in the United States and in Cuba, but also I refer to an ongoing conversation among Latinos, Latinas and Latin Americans. I am not talking about a utopia here; the conversation is already taking place, or must be taking place, at least in our classrooms, which I will return to later.

It is now a commonplace to say that the United States is becoming a Latin nation. That may be, but more important than census statistics is the answer to this question: what kind of nation might that be? Whatever the answer, the fact is that individuals like Martí should figure prominently in the culture of the United States. By "figuring" I do not mean inclusion in a Latin *Who's Who*. I do mean inclusion in the curricula of our teaching institutions not only as a "representative man" but also as part of serious scholarship and debate. Such an inclusion requires arduous work: translation, interpretation, critical thinking, and teaching. Educational bureaucrats insist that our curricula must become "diverse," a favorite buzzword. But diversity as smorgasbord is at best quaint, at worst ridiculous if not downright insulting. Critical inclusion means dialogue among texts, for example between Martí and Emerson, the subject of chapter five, but also between Martí and Du Bois or Martí and Dickinson.

These equestrian statues in Central Park recall the Spanish American wars of independence and celebrate heroic deeds whose immediacy has faded, their glory and their pain forever erased from living memory. Feeling not at all heroic but rather addled by everything around me, I stand in front of the statue of Martí, flanked by the other two heroes: Bolívar and San Martín, nation builders of colossal proportions, grand figures in Latin America's historical narrative. Martí was a journalist and a poet who became a national hero. He was in fact a poet and a philosopher, and above all, a lover of wisdom: *philosophia*. Wisdom is another one of those words worn by time. There is something stony about it. Its adjective has long been degraded in "wise guy," a charlatan. Yet in the whirlwind that was his life, Martí became wise in an ancient, nearly lost sense. He became a knower of things human and divine, and of the ways that these things could be made to work for the betterment of humankind. That was his project for Cuba and for Latin America. He died before he could see it fail, but to this day the radiance of his effort remains. It remains not only because of Martí's political genius but also because he was a modern visionary, a comrade-in-arms "of Lautréamont and Rimbaud, a descendent of Baudelaire, a precursor of the modern travelers to hell. That is to say, he belongs to the poetic legacy that best interpreted the terrible annihilating process of modernity" (Rama 197). It may seem contradictory that Martí was an Emersonian and a "descendent of Baudelaire," as Rama argues. Emerson's best know dictum was the betterment of humankind; Baudelaire was the prototypical, modern "traveler to hell." Martí took from both, incorporating the contradiction in a way that echoed the expansive voice of that other American Martí also admired, Walt Whitman: "Yo vengo de todas partes,/ Y hacia todas partes voy" (I come from all places/ and to all places go) (*Selected Writings* 272). Moreover, in *El poeta y la ciudad* (the poet and the city), Spanish poet Dionisio Cañas writes that in Martí, one finds the "essential elements that will later be recycled (and modified) by almost all of the Hispanic poets who have subsequently passed through the North American metropolis" (51).

Writings on the life and works of Martí have ranged from early biographies, notably Jorge Mañach's seminal *Martí el apóstol* (Martí the Apostle) (1933), to recent readings that portray him as a keen observer in the teeming city of New York. The title of one of the sections in *José Martí's "Our America,"* a collection of critical essays published in 1998, refers to Martí as a "Latino outsider," a surprising yet remarkably apt term. For many years now, there has been in the United States sustained if modest interest in Martí and his works. Mañach's 1933 biography, translated by Coley Taylor as *Martí, Apostle of Freedom*, was published in 1950. There have been several selected anthologies of his works translated into English with varying degrees of success. In 2002, Penguin Classics published *The Selected Writings of José Martí*, translated and edited by Esther Allen. Along with more familiar works, such as "Our America," this excellent anthology includes many works never before translated, notably Martí's *War Diaries*, published in English in their entirety for the first time. Important critical works written in Spanish, for example by Julio Ramos, have been translated into English. Yet Martí and his works remain marginal to contemporary culture in the United States. In fact, Martí's legacy should be central to our contemporary debates on identity, on "race" relations, on the role of the United States in world politics and on value and meaning, some of the topics addressed in these pages.

Cuba has of course claimed Martí as a national hero, a process that intensified after the revolution of 1933 when "rebellious nationalism was the keynote of the new spirit" (Aguilar 71). As Ette has shown, after Cuba's 1959 revolution, the saintly halo placed around Martí's head by some of his early panegyrists was replaced by readings that emphasized Martí as a radical revolutionary, consistently critical of the expanding might of the United States. On the other hand, exiled critics have insisted that Martí's defense of democracy was proof that readings by socialist critics had a political agenda that was alien to Martí's defense of democratic ideals. The fact is that there have been excellent readings of Martí from many different angles, conducted in many latitudes, along with reams of ephemeral, inconsequential commentaries. Be that as it may, the impasses in the politics of Cuba and the United States in the last forty years have produced a correlative impasse in certain areas of Martí scholarship. As already mentioned, the standoff has been summarized in Ette's study of Martí's reception as well as in John M. Kirk's *José Martí: Mentor of the Cuban Nation* and in Enrico Mario Santí's "José Martí and the Cuban Revolution." One can only hope that new approaches to Martí and his works, in the United States and in Cuba, continue to reconsider his writings in ways that are more pertinent to contemporary culture and politics. It is obvious that for students of Cuba, the figure of Martí has long been a focal point. It should be no less obvious that for students of the United States, especially in the period known as the Gilded Age, Martí's works offer a unique point of view and perhaps a fresh point of departure. The thoughtful, if brief, entry on Martí in *Gotham: A History of New York City to 1898* (Burrows and Wallace) should be expanded.

Martí believed that the sovereignty of a nation guaranteed the rights of its citizens, but he mistrusted the flag-waving nationalism of the demagogue. He believed that all nations should share in a vision of universal harmony. Today such an idea may seem as naïve as the pipe dream of a belated romantic, but for Martí it held real promise. He believed in democratic ideals, but from his vantage point in New York City he also saw quite a different picture of a working democracy. Martí's gaze on New York and on the politics and culture of the United States was sustained for 15 of his most productive years. That unblinking eye reflects the culture of the metropolis like none other before and perhaps none other since. It is a founding gaze that gives us a sharp evaluation of the best and the worst that the United States has to offer.

Generations of Cuban school children have learned the story of Martí's self-sacrificing life and heroic death. Martí's features, distorted for aesthetic effect, are a constant presence wherever Cubans have gathered, from Havana's huge Revolution Square to a corner of Miami's Little Havana. In Cuba, town squares and country schools are proud of their "Martí corner," a secular altar to the nation's hero. In bronze, marble, and more often in the plaster of Paris of a bibelot, reproduction has turned Martí's visage into an almost kitsch icon of nationhood. Yet as a writer Martí still has a great deal to offer, especially for us Latinos and Latinas, as we cobble together on this side of the Río Bravo a new culture with tensions and creative possibilities all its own. Martí's eye on New York and the culture of the United States counters the alienated and alienating gaze that might turn us into politically useful props or into the "cultural" flavor of the month, exotic, disposable pieces of someone else's puzzle.

Martí's thoughts on wealth, on race, on eminent North Americans, on the expanding role of the United States, on death and transcendence were newly hewn in New York City. Martí used the term "Latins"—*los latinos, la gente latina*—to underline the common links among Cubans, Puerto Ricans, Dominicans, Mexicans and other Latin Americans who supported his efforts to liberate Cuba. At times the style of Martí's writing may seem as distant from today as the steam locomotive and the telegraph. Yet on many issues, Martí's words are sharp and fresh, certainly more powerful in their way than the ready-made prattle coming at us from every angle.

In writing about Martí, my goal has been to open a place for the kind of dialogue that goes on or should go on in a classroom. Today authority has become a synonym of oppression. We are rightfully fearful of masterful posturings, of politicos who lay exclusive claim to righteousness and values. Martí wrote about righteousness and values, but he stood solidly on the side of the weak, the dispossessed and the disenfranchised. Yet Martí's writing is not about victims but about power, which can be harnessed through wisdom. Today it seems that learning is often reduced to statistics, to tests required for admission and exams designed to measure the knowledge of those eager to move on to "the real world." In a frequent complaint of educators and reformers, it is said that the classroom has become as subject to the demands of the marketplace as a factory or an auction house. Martí offers a hopeful and useful counter-argument. For him the classroom is a privileged space, the core of what used to be called "civilization," which to him did not mean elitism and exclusion but uninhibited cooperation across every false boundary conjured by the human mind. The classroom encompasses and transcends the privacy of the home and the duties of the public sphere. For Martí, it is the place where people learn to tolerate and love one another in a way that may be powerful and revolutionary. Martí taught in various institutions in New York City, and the role of education is central in his ideological agenda. In 1890 Martí and Rafael Serra (1858- 1909), also exiled in New York, founded a new school called *La Liga* (the league), where "whites and blacks may sit together" (donde se sientan juntos blancos y negros) (González Veranés 18).

Martí came to New York in January, 1880 at the age of 27. Like "a dark monster," the brand-new elevated roared down Ninth Avenue, frightening horses and showering sparks of coal dust. Although he traveled frequently, New York City was Martí's home base for the next 15 years. New York might have been something of a home, as much of a home as an exile can make in the great city. Martí's goal was a heroic return to Cuban soil, which was, if not home, certainly the only patria he ever wanted. New York was the awesome capital of wealth he inhabited out of necessity. Yet the city offered a place to work and a refuge, however precarious and transitory.

Martí left New York for the last time on January 30, 1895, on board the steamer *Athos*, sailing south toward Haiti. He spent his last birthday, January 28, hiding at a friend's house on West 65th Street, fearful that his plans might be again discovered and destroyed. Earlier that month, United States authorities had stopped an expedition that was ready to sail from the coast of Florida, not far from Jacksonville. Arms and supplies were confiscated. Devastated by this disastrous failure, Martí nevertheless gathered new resources and managed to organize a second expedition to land in Cuba and rekindle the unfinished struggle for its independence from Spain, the waning empire more desperate than ever to hold on to its treasure islands. Martí was killed in battle about five weeks after his arrival in the province of Oriente, on May 19, less than four months after he left New York.

As noted by many readers, Martí's New York years are at the core of his life and his work. To support himself and his family, he wrote. He wrote, it seems, about everything and everyone during his years in the city he called "The Iron Babel," in honor of its architecture and its status as the colossal entry to legions of immigrants. In 1883, three years after Martí's arrival in the city, the Brooklyn Bridge opened, a spectacular achievement celebrated by thousands of people. Martí was there, holding his young son on his shoulders, over the heads of the jubilant crowd. Coney Island dazzled visitors with garlands of electric lights and unheard-of marvels: Martí was there, alone in the crowd. Criminal trials, labor strikes, art exhibits, political turmoil, elections, the death of a poet, the assassination of a president, a funeral in Chinatown, the latest feats of reconstructive surgery: Martí covered all these topics and then some.

In articles published all over Latin American, Martí wrote on Emerson, Whitman, Longfellow, Grant, Buffalo Bill and Jesse James. In *José Martí and U.S. Writers*, Anne Fountain has identified references to dozens of writers, from the well-known essay on Emerson to a brief mention in 1882 of Henry James, "a young novelist," fond of the style of the French (9:18). Martí also wrote about Henry Garnet, "notable Negro orator," the son of runaway slaves who became United States ambassador to Liberia. No other Latin American writer knew the glories and the shames of the United States as well as Martí. He wrote in awe of the democratic process and in horror of other forces that were transforming the city and the nation into a Darwinian nightmare.

For Martí, Coney Island became an emblem of the nation at the end of the nineteenth century: a fun house, a hall of mirrors, placating the many with sights and sounds never before conceived, presided over by a magician whose sleight of hand seemed to make poverty, racism and spiritual abjection disappear. Chapter one, entitled "Coney Island: Alone in a Crowd," focuses on Martí's essays on the great amusement park, newly opened on what had been a nearly deserted stretch of beach.

In his essays on Coney Island, Martí contrasts the breathless admiration of the press for the razzle-dazzle of the world's greatest amusement park with emerging values and new codes of behavior that he found troubling. Anticipating the jeremiads of later critics, Martí saw how social injustice and spiritual poverty were masked in a newly created culture of "amusement for the millions." In the process, he portrays himself as a lone prophet, crying not in the wilderness but in a sea of humanity.

Martí marveled at the wealth of New York City but wearied of the city's infatuation with luxury. A few years before Thorstein Veblen published *The Theory of the Leisure Class* (1899), in which he coined the expression "conspicuous consumption," Martí looked in disbelief as New York's "Anglomaniacal rascals" (bellacos anglómanos) showed off their wealth with lackeys in full livery, buckles on their shoes, silk stockings and red frock coats (13:436). The vain display of luxury brings with it a chilly harshness that turns neighbors into spectators, Martí writes. In some of his essays, he contrasts what he calls the "primitive" spirit of the nation with a newly acquired hunger for luxury and pomp. Charmed by the getting and spending of the well-heeled, newly arrived immigrants threw themselves into the endless task of accumulating wealth and the listless enjoyment of their new fortunes. People of modest means were enticed to hock their souls for the sake of displaying cheap versions of the trappings of wealth. This is the sickness eating at the greatness of this nation, Martí writes. Martí was no ascetic, and he had no use for the fire-and-brimstone rhetoric of puritanical preachers. As he fought tirelessly for Cuba's independence, he struggled to make things comfortable for himself and his family. Without reasonable prosperity, he said, life can be bitter, but without the joys of the spirit, wealth becomes a bloated carcass on a gilded bier.

Martí's writings are a warning to any newcomer who might too easily and too uncritically imitate the values and customs of an emerging consumer culture, divorced from what Martí saw as the moral core of a nation, a respect for freedom and equality. He warned his Latin readers, without resorting to the cliché that all that glitters is not gold, that our stores of spirit are a treasure to be unearthed and cherished. His voice still pleads that we search for those sources and use them.

In the crowds at Coney Island, the sight of women walking alone especially troubled Martí. By the time he strolled down the huge boardwalk, reformers of the period were referring to the area as "Sodom by the sea." Parts of the area had initially been settled by transients, petty criminals, women and men "of easy virtue." There was a climate of sexual promiscuity that scandalized religious and civic leaders and their constituents. The new Coney Island was the work of entrepreneurial hucksters; it was also a great democratic experiment in providing rest and relaxation for the masses. Racial segregation had already been accomplished, not only in the South but throughout the North as well. The amusement park now provided a microcosmic prototype of a society segregated by class. On the other hand, the lines of demarcation would remain fluid and porous to some degree, a characteristic quality of American democracy that would allow for radical divisions among different classes while preserving a semblance of the democratic spirit.

In the newly built Coney Island, respectable, well-to-do citizens could dine in elegant restaurants, while the crowds enjoyed their home-cooked picnic on the beach. If the fringes of this society offered fluidity and transgression, specifically in the area of sexual activity and gender identity, in the central spaces, gender roles were radically polarized. In this world, the woman walking alone was an outsider if not an outcast, a troubling by-product of the rigid, heterosexual symmetry offered by the Victorian couple. It is in this context that one must consider Martí's own reading of the gender polarities of the period, the subject of the chapter titled "The New Woman and the Anxieties of Gender."

In Martí's magazine for children, *La Edad de Oro* (the golden years) and in his poetry, gender roles are polarized according to the rigid binarism of the times. In the magazine for children, little girls are told that they are the mothers of tomorrow, while little boys will grow up to be virtuous "gentlemen." Some of Martí's poetry replays the topic of "Frailty, thy name is woman," that is, physically delicate and thus attractive to a man, as well as morally weak and thus potentially dangerous to his "virility." In other writings by Martí, the binary man-woman becomes a contrast between "masculinity" and "femininity," defined as moral, cultural and even aesthetic categories not always bound to a biologically determined gender. In other words, a dose of what is delicate and feminine is a worthy quality in man, provided it does not compromise his virility.

On the other hand, in the United States Martí witnessed the beginnings of radical changes in the role of women. In his perceptive comments on the early women's movement, he contrasts the conventional role of women as delicate virgins and saintly mothers with the changing roles played by "the new woman." With a sense of awe and unease, Martí considered aspects of these new roles, from the sad plight of the exploited factory "girl" to the powerful oratory of new female leaders. Martí is explicit in his defense of the rights of women to equal wages, but in other settings he returns to the "sacred" image of woman as mother and companion, or to its dreaded counterpart as deceitful temptress.

For Martí "man" never ceases to be a universal category, one still very much in use, especially by Latin writers, who to this day write annoyingly of *el hombre* (man) as the equivalent of "humankind." However, Martí also posits the category of "workers of the mind," which encompasses men and women. In a remarkable juxtaposition, he contrasts the Biblical narrative of Adam and Eve with a native narrative in which both "man" and "woman" issue from the very same "seed."

Martí believed fervently in democratic ideals, but he also saw those ideals unraveling around him. He understood the reasons for the fearful tearing at the fabric of the republic, and he knew that chief among them was the question of race and race prejudice. Martí's understanding of race, his criticism of racism in the United States, and his struggle against the racist elements in Cuba's struggle for independence are the topics covered in chapter three, "Against Race." The phrase is taken from the title of a book by Paul Gilroy, whose subtitle, *Imagining Political Culture beyond the Color Line*, is an apt description of Martí's own anti-racist project. The historical reality of "race" and the all-too-evident manifestations of contemporary race-hatred were staring Martí in the face every day of his life. His rhetorical appeal to put at end to race-thinking was politically motivated, but it was also a way to imagine, and to invite others to imagine what might be possible "beyond the color line." The impact of Martí's anti-racist thinking and its inevitable contradictions are the subject of Alejandro de la Fuente's *A Nation for All: Race, Inequality and Politics in Twentieth-Century Cuba*.

Briefly put, Martí believed that race prejudice, whatever forms it might take, whatever excuse might be used to justify it, had no place in a democracy. Martí feared for the United States, where he saw racism thriving like a weed. He feared that if Cuba remained divided by its own prejudices, it would never be a democratic republic. In Cuba and in the United States, Martí witnessed the abominable treatment of people of African descent. In New York he learned of the military campaigns designed to push the native people of the North American continent to the abject edges of the nation. In his own body, he felt the sting of misunderstanding, disdain and exclusion.

After arriving in New York City and during travels to Tampa and Key West, Martí witnessed the deplorable situation of African Americans in *el norte*. He wrote with great sympathy and compassion about their struggle to make good on the promise of emancipation. He implored all Cubans to unite in the struggle against the tyranny of racism. By 1893, when Martí wrote his most famous essay on the topic, "Mi raza" (my race), race prejudice was the norm in the United States. Indeed, ten years earlier in 1883, the Supreme Court had struck down the Civil Rights Act of 1875, opening the door for the "legal" segregation of public institutions. In 1896, in *Plessy vs. Ferguson*, the Supreme Court rule that "racial segregation" mandated by the states did not violate the Constitution's equal protection clause (Eric Foner 132). Martí's years in the United States, 1880–1895, are framed by these two historical decisions. All people of color, Native Americans, Latin people and people of African descent were consigned to various legal, scientific and cultural tiers, all inferior to the Anglo-Saxon race, a newly manufactured category, the only arbiter of its own "superiority." This is part of the setting of Martí's "My Race."

Martí was a pioneer in considering "race" as a category created to oppress people. When he famously said "there are no races," he was referring to the artificial nature of the practice of classifying human beings according to their external physical characteristics. Martí deplored the use of such classifications to deny people equal treatment in the legal system and to block their access to various institutions, notably those associated with education and public life. Martí did not ignore cultural differences among people; on the contrary, he embraced them, for example, writing with great admiration about the art of the people native to the American continent. He did indeed write "against race" when "race" was used as a category for determining the status of a citizen.

With uncompromising zeal, Martí envisioned a democratic republic ruled by the sacred tenets of the enlightenment: equality, liberty, fraternity. The republic, like the famous representation of justice, must be color-blind, as indeed it is in the founding documents of a democratic nation. I write this on January 20, 2003, the day that honors the birthday of Dr. Martin Luther King, Jr. I pause to watch King deliver his "I Have a Dream" speech on television. One day, he says, his children "will not be judged by the color of their skin but the content of their character," an uncanny echo of Martí's words. "Blacks, as well as whites, are divided according to their character" ("Los negros, como los blancos, se dividen por sus caracteres") Martí writes in "My Race" (2:299).

Chapter four, entitled "Pan-Americanism's Empty Train," deals with Martí's participation in the Pan-American Congress of 1889, held in Washington, D.C. Some of the facts about the congress and Martí's role in it provide the context for a discussion of Martí's "Nuestra América" (our America), perhaps his most famous, most influential essay. Beginning in the fall of 1889, the United States and the Latin American nations met in Washington to consider economic and political issues that affected the entire hemisphere. Eager to impress the Latin nations, the government of the United States chartered a luxurious train that took delegates on a grand tour of the nation, covering some five thousand miles. The train proved to be a public relations disaster, domestically and internationally. Nevertheless, it achieved its goal in displaying advances in technology and comfort never before seen by most of the delegates.

The New York press called the train "a Juggernaut," referring to the mythical cart that crushed everything in its path. If the metaphor is crude, its message is clear: Get on board or get crushed. Each Latin American nation brought its own agenda to Washington, and its delegates were unlikely to fall in line behind Martí, in spite of his prestigious position as consul of Uruguay, Argentina and Paraguay in New York. On the other hand, as a delegate to the congress, Martí underscored the fact that for the United States, hemispheric unity was less about transnational cooperation than about insuring its central position in the economic and political future of the Latin nations. As Martí saw it, delegates were literally being taken for a ride in a fancy train, and he said so in no uncertain terms. Not all Latin delegates had chosen to make the journey, but many of those who did began to leave it along the way, embarrassed by the political fallout. By the time the train went through Richmond on its way back to Washington, it was empty.

Martí's project was not only to liberate Cuba from Spanish domination but also to transform the island colony into a democratic republic.

Through his tireless activism and through his writing, he lay the foundations for such a republic. Martí's admiration for democracy in the United States, for the richness of the country's resources, for its boundless energy, for its writers, orators and reformers, is evident in many of his writings. However, Martí was also a witness to the radical alteration and at times the destruction of democratic ideals on many fronts. He wrote with vision about such a transformation, as a warning to those whose awe at the technological brilliance and boundless wealth of *el norte* might lead them to an uncritical imitation. The warning still stands.

To borrow the title of Andrew Delbanco's book, Martí should be one of our "required readings." Writing in late–nineteenth-century New York, he seems at times to speak directly to the present. "That evening," he writes in one of his notebooks, "from my bedroom window, half naked, I saw the sprawling city and caught a glimpse of the future, thinking of Emerson" (22:323). These words are not found in the essays Martí published in prestigious journals; they are notes, scribbled on bits of paper, offering a maddening task to generations of editors. The awkward placing of the participle, "thinking of Emerson," may or may not be deliberate. At any rate, if the syntax is unpolished, the image is still suggestive. Martí's vision of the future, though inspired by Emerson, is not grounded on the rather orderly countryside around Concord but seems to float over the huge city. From its vantage point, this "half naked" body, all but lost in the metropolis, is still capable of vision, though a fleeting, partial one: "entreví lo futuro"—"I caught a glimpse of the future."

The portrait of Martí that emerges from his best known works emphasizes moral character and artistic perception: I am a sincere man, I see, I am afraid. In the fragment on Emerson I have just mentioned, there is a rare glimpse of Martí's body, of his private space, his most intimate vulnerability, his mind at work. In that moment a meditation on Emerson, perhaps the writer Martí most admired, informs a vision of the city, sprawling, exhausted, *la ciudad postrada*. It is an image reflected in the gaze of this eminent outsider and projected towards the future, which is our present. Though imbedded in a maze of notes and fragments, this passage resonates throughout Martí's works. Any new reading should profit from its suggestion of a vital connection that defies time and space.

In chapter five, entitled "Bilingual Emerson," I review Martí's debt to "the Sage of Concord." While writing this chapter, I realized how much of my work on Martí involved translation, in the sense of rendering one language into another, but also in a sense that my dictionary includes

under the subheading "telegraphy," that is, translation as "the retrans-
mitting or forwarding of a message, as by relay."

Translation as rendering one language into another may be the exile's
first, and in some cases endless, burden. It is assumed at an early
age when a clever child, fairly proficient in the language of Emerson,
interprets for a befuddled father, still wearing his nationality, to play
on a Puerto Rican saying, like a yarmulke at an Irish wedding. In the
telegraphic sense, the sense I want to latch on to, translation offers a
soothing participation in that "relay," in this case Martí's Emersonian
bilingual web. Martí's essay on Emerson is criticism but it is also a mul-
tilayered work of translation, not only from English into Spanish but also
within Spanish, in order to reproduce not just Emerson's ideas but an
Emersonian style in Spanish. This is the process admirably described by
Cuban critic Gustavo Pérez-Firmat when, in *The Cuban Condition*, he
discusses the emergence of original works from "the translation of
exogenous models and forms" (5).

Every Cuban school child knows something about Martí's death,
the final scene in a heroic legend indelibly written in Cuba's national
consciousness. Death and transcendence are the topics of the chapter
six, "Martí Faces Death." This title was inspired by Andrew
Delbanco's essay "Throreau Faces Death," included in *Required
Reading: Why Our American Classics Matter Now*. There are admiring
mentions of Throreau in Martí's work, but Martí reserved his greatest admiration, condensed in a dazzling eulogy, for another famous
New Englander, Ralph Waldo Emerson, Thoreau's neighbor and his
moral, philosophical alter ego. Yet like Thoreau, Martí sought to
come to terms with a death that he surely foresaw in his final days in
the backwoods of eastern Cuba. To quote Delbanco quoting
Thoreau, Martí struggled "to keep from flinching as 'the sweet edge'
of death [cut] him 'through the heart and marrow'" (*Required Reading*
44).

After years of struggle and failure, Martí finally succeeded in organizing a small expedition that would enter Cuba at its eastern end and begin
making contacts with local opposition to Spanish rule. Along with
Dominican general Máximo Gómez and a handful of supporters, Martí
landed in a remote beach not far from Guantánamo. After some five
weeks on the move, through hills and thickets, the insurrectionists made
their way to the heart of Cuba's Oriente region, camping near Dos Ríos.
Around noon on May 19 1895, against orders issued by General Gómez
to keep away from the frontlines, Martí charged toward the enemy. A
lone aide, uncannily named Angel de la Guardia (guardian angel), followed close behind. Minutes later, Martí was shot by a Spanish sniper

hiding in the underbrush. A Cuban scout, working for the Spanish authorities, finished him off with his Remington rifle. Martí's doomed charge is captured in the statue in New York's Central Park. Angel de la Guardia was wounded but survived to tell Gómez, and history, what had happened.

Immortalized in marble and bronze, endlessly evoked in the speeches of patriots and politicians, described by critics and panegyrists, the image of Martí's heroic death is silent and garrulous at the same time. The statue topping a granite monolith says one thing: heroism. The words woven around that act rework the same story in endless versions, rife with commonplaces: that Martí staged his own death to defy those who accused him of inaction, that he opted for a noble death that would seal his standing in the nation's memory, that he now lives in words forever charged by an act of patriotic sacrifice. More to the point may be the fact that Martí had no military training to speak of. Other accounts of the incidents of May 19 point to the chaos and confusion of battle, which caused Martí to find himself alone in a clearing. Whatever the facts, Martí's heroic death is a founding scene in Cuba's national myth, and as such, it defies interpretation even as it invites the endless work of memorializing. Martí's *War Diaries*, the texts that record the events leading to that heroic death, are a different story, or rather a series of stories, taken up in the last chapter.

Martí's diary is a visionary's last stance. It captures the moment when every plant, every bite of food and every human gesture are perceived anew, charged by an ineffable wisdom and a knowledge not beyond words but refracted through them as through a prism. Martí's diary is the final chapter in a life lived in the knowledge of death. The statement must sound odd to many of us. It hardly bears repeating that despite a recent awakening on the subject of death, very little in our everyday life prepares us for that inevitable event. The recommendation of the ancients, paraphrased by writer Lezama Lima, that nothing is wiser or healthier than a daily meditation on death, is alien to most of us. Religious faith certainly prepares us for death, but Martí wanted a secular wisdom about death that might be incorporated into the fabric of the republic and embraced by all, regardless of individual religious beliefs or lack of them.

Coney Island as a microcosm of a new metropolis, gender-based qualities and the changing role of women, the evils of racism, the ways to counter the might of a rising empire, translating Emerson, the wisdom found on the eve of death. These are the aspects of Martí's work discussed in this book. These topics represent the limits of my interests and my research. Martí's work is richer than these pages could possibly suggest. I offer them as a point of departure, especially for those first encountering Martí's work. To those who have already been there, they may offer new insights or new points of disagreement. They may rekindle old debates or suggest new ones. Though it is a commonplace to say so, it is true that Martí's work cannot be reduced to a single volume or a library full of them. Rather his corpus offers a symbolic space, the classroom I referred to earlier, open to all and especially welcoming to the informed dissent that is the prelude to democratic dialogue.

CHAPTER 1

CONEY ISLAND: ALONE IN A CROWD

Is the United States the greatest nation in the world or the greatest show on earth? This is the question Martí put before his readers after his visit to Coney Island, not long after his arrival in New York City. Substance versus appearance, compassion versus greed, sacrifice versus pleasure, depth of spirit versus shallow optimism, the common good versus common interests. Martí wanted to show his readers the force of these dualities at the heart of the culture of the United States. He presented such contrasts not as bookish abstractions but in the carnival of humanity of an amusement park, newly built on the edge of the city. He wanted to bring his readers an image of the dazzling extravaganza by the beach, but he also wanted them to cast a critical eye on a place exclusively designed for "amusing the million[s]," a popular phrase used later as the title of John Kasson's 1978 book about Coney Island. Coney Island dazzled the visitor, but Martí also saw it as the place of an unsettling "dismemberment of traditional community" (Ramos 195). Through the spectacle of Coney Island, Martí set out to define a Latin difference, a narrative of Latin spirituality to counter the extravagant materialism of the North. It is a simplistic formula, but it worked. Its fallout is still with us.

By the time Martí wrote about it, Coney Island had already acquired the infamous epithet of "Sodom by the sea." A 1941 book by Oliver Pilat used the phrase in its title, softening it with the subtitle: "An Affectionate History of Coney Island." A review of Pilat's *Sodom by the Sea* was harsher in its judgment, calling the book "a history of American vulgarity." Toward the end of the century, Pilat wrote, not a Sunday passed during the summer without a couple of "blistering sermons" about Coney Island (117). Martí's writings about Coney Island have less of the fire-and-brimstone of the pulpit and something much closer to a reflective unease provoked by the spectacle before him. Martí's "Coney Island" is closer to a meditation than to a sermon, though something of the reformer's outrage lingers in its pages.

Martí's vision of Coney Island is closer to John Kasson's critical reading of the amusement park as a "symbol of the new cultural order" than to the weekly jeremiads of nineteenth-century preachers. In Coney Island, Martí, like Kasson, saw a "harbinger of modernity." In the spectacle of Coney Island, Martí witnessed a withering of treasured values: human love and cooperation, a reverence for nature, and the equanimity to reflect on them. Martí saw Coney Island less as a spectacle than as a ruin, and he needed new ways of looking, and of writing, to bear witness to the glories and the catastrophes of modernity. As an exile, Martí inhabited a "shattered home," critic Julio Ramos has written. Martí needed to recast himself in a new place, "the house of discourse," which is to say, he had to write his way out of the chaos he witnessed. He had to bear witness, so that others after him might make use of the fragmented wisdom he pieced together, not the genteel outrage of the reformer but the critical eye of a shrewd observer.

Martí arrived in New York on the third of January 1880, on a mail steamer coming from the French port of Le Havre. The year before he had once again been banished from Cuba for conspiring against the colonial government. He was deported to Spain, but after a brief stay there, he escaped to France, then made his way to New York, where he would eventually organize the struggle for Cuba's independence. He was 27 years old, with a wife and a baby son to support. In some notes for a "speech in English," Martí wrote in that language, "But if I am unable to speak pardonable English, I am [at] least able and most willing, to bear witness" (23:327). Whatever his proficiency in the language of Emerson, Martí's willingness to bear witness became the driving force behind his extensive writings about the United States.

Martí had one goal that towered above all others: Cuba's freedom. In hundreds of articles and public speeches, he sought support for the cause of independence. But he also had to support himself and his family, and help the rest of his family back in Cuba. The same year he arrived in New York, he published articles in English in the magazine *The Hour* and wrote for the *Sun*, published by the formidable Charles A. Dana (1819–1897). However, he wrote most extensively about North American culture for Latin American newspapers, as well as for Latin readers in the United States. In his writings about the United States, Martí handled political and cultural intricacies with the ease of an insider; yet he never lost the critical eye of the outsider. Martí traveled frequently, but for 15 years, from 1880 to 1895, his base of operations was in New York City. His position remained paradoxical, not a bad place for a critical observer of the culture and politics of the United States.

Soon after his arrival, the tone of Martí's vision of the United States was set not in the heart of the city but on its fringe, in Coney Island, a place certainly like no other Martí had ever seen. "In the annals of human history, there is no equal to the marvelous prosperity of the United States," Martí writes, echoing the admiration of local newspapers. Yet he immediately gives the outline of a counter-argument to this unbridled admiration. Like a first-rate journalist, Martí wanted his readers to make up their own minds; but like a good teacher, he also wanted to nudge them in the right direction.

Martí's descriptions of the happy crowd at the seaside are full of color and movement. In Martí's writings about Coney Island, there is also something of the ambivalent fascination that the place would provoke in later generations of writers and artists. Newspaper articles of the period tried to capture the spirit of the place in hyperbolic descriptions, but with characteristic prescience, Martí found that only a rapid montage could do it justice. Coney Island was a place "brimming with people, filled with luxurious hotels, crossed by an elevated train, brightened with gardens, booths, small theatres, beer halls, circuses, tents, hordes of carriages, picturesque assemblies, food carts, grocers, fountains" ("rebosante de gente, sembrado de suntuosos hoteles, cruzado de un ferrocarril aéreo, matizado de jardines, de kioscos, de pequeños teatros, de cervecerías, de circos, de tiendas de campaña, de masas de carruajes, de asambleas pintorescas, de casillas ambulantes, de vendutas, de fuentes") (9:123).

All of this had risen from a pile of sand, turned into a Mecca for people from all over the city and all over the country. Martí added numbers and statistics to a panoramic view of a huge crowd, unlike any he or any of his readers had ever seen. The dining room of one of the hotels could easily accommodate 4,000 people. Indeed, the spectacle lent itself to hyperbole: one hotel seemed to hold an entire nation. In fact, the entire nation seemed poised to pass through the gates of Coney Island. During the 1870s, Manhattan Beach, Brighton Beach and West Brighton were quickly developed. By 1878, as many as 60,000 people came to the beach on a summer day. On July 5, 1887, a front-page article in the *Sun* declared that 100,000 "patriotic pleasure seekers" had visited Coney Island to celebrate the Fourth of July.

Of the four beaches, West Brighton, which Martí calls Gable, was the best. An elevator, taller than the spire of Trinity Church, and twice as tall as the Cathedral in Havana, carried people up to the sky in a fragile cage. New York had not yet become the city of skyscrapers, and the elevator at West Brighton must have been quite a sight. No less impressive were Gable's piers, networks of iron thrust into the ocean for the length of three blocks. One hotel, formerly a pavilion at the Philadelphia Exposition (1876), had been brought in pieces and reassembled at the beach.

Gable Beach had museums that exhibited "human monsters, extravagant fish, bearded ladies, melancholy dwarfs, and rickety elephants" ("monstruos humanos, peces extravagantes, mujeres barbudas, enanos melancólicos, y elefantes raquíticos") billed as "the biggest elephants in the world" (9:124). Behind Martí's words, one can almost hear the harsh twang of the carnival barker. With the mention of the rickety elephants, Martí's admiring view of Coney Island begins to shift. Something is not right, Martí seems to be saying. "The biggest elephants in the world" of the poster are in fact "rickety elephants." The image of the elephants provokes other questions. Who are these "human monsters" people pay to see? Why are they exhibited? Why are the dwarfs melancholy? The questions remain unanswered, opening the door to other aspects of Coney Island that trouble the visitor. Licit and illicit pleasures flourished at the beach, and Martí wrote of the sense of loneliness and alienation that they provoked in him. He saved his fiercest outrage, however, for the most devastating "social vice": poverty, a condition that is not merely the lack of fortune but deprivation in the midst of plenty, hunger and abjection disguised in a carnival of plenty.

Before antibiotics, before sick people were sealed in air-conditioned cubicles, it was common wisdom that sun and fresh air could improve health and cure certain illnesses. But the open air alone could not cure a summer plague that killed hundreds of children. In the frolicking gaiety of the beach, Martí saw the signs of cholera, a disease especially associated with the lack of hygiene and the overcrowding of urban poverty. It is a disease that is most deadly among children, which explains the name used by Martí, *cholera infantum*. Martí wrote of "unfortunate toddlers, who seem as if devoured, as if sucked and gnawed from the inside by that terrible summer illness that cuts down children like the scythe mows down wheat" (desventurados pequeñuelos, que parecen como devorados, como chupados, como roídos, por esa terrible enfermedad de verano que siega niños como la hoz siega la mies) (9:124). The image of sick children, taken to the seashore in a futile effort to heal them, is still a disturbing image, its impact highlighted by the din of the crowd at the carnival by the shore. The good intentions of philanthropists might have given poor, sick children a day at the beach, but it did nothing to address the appalling conditions in which they lived during the rest of the year.

Like no other Latin American writer, Martí saw the New York of Jacob Riis in the gaiety at Coney Island. He gave his readers the sunny,

postcard reality expected of a travel writer, but he could not leave out a
dose of a different kind of reality. Jacob Riis (1849–1914), a Danish
immigrant who settled in New York, photographed the underside of the
city: airless cubicles packed with haggard immigrants, sweat shops and
homeless children roaming the filthy streets of the Lower East Side.
Riis's book, *How the Other Half Lives*, first published in 1890, brought
almost instant attention to the squalor of New York's tenements and
promoted significant reforms in housing, education and child-labor
laws. Like Riis, Martí saw the other side of the pretty postcard that was
Coney Island, and he shared his vision with his Latin readers.

There is comfort in nostalgia, and the last years of the nineteenth century have long been a source of images of a quaint past. In his writings
about Coney Island and New York City, Martí captured something of
that world: cast iron piers glistening in a golden light, rows of elegant
carriages, lovers on the boardwalk. Women rented blue flannel bathing
suits and straw hats; men, in simpler suits, took them by the hand and
ran toward the waves. Children filled their little buckets with sand,
screaming with delight at the coming of the waves.

Yet something was not right. Coney Island was called a "summer
safety valve" for the crowded city, and there was indeed something
mechanical about the regimented gaiety it offered. Human beings have
long gathered to trade, buy and sell, to worship and to share each other's
company. In the great expositions of the nineteenth century, people
came to admire new inventions and displays from distant cultures. At
Coney Island something entirely new was taking place. Hordes of people went there for the sole purpose of enjoying a day's amusement. As
John Kasson explains in *Amusing the Million*, at the end of the nineteenth century the United States began a transition from an economy
organized around production to one organized around consumption
(101). This is precisely the transition that amazed and troubled Martí,
and he conveyed something of his state of mind as the first Latin
American to witness such a transformation. Martí grappled with a vision
he could barely put into writing. But put it in writing he did, and the
tension of the effort is richly evident.

There was more to Martí's unease in Coney Island than the prim
objections of a genteel reformer, shocked at a new code of conduct that
surely signaled a major shift in the sexual mores of North American culture. As we read him today, there is more to his vision that the shock of
a newly arrived immigrant at the first American beach party. What
most troubled Martí was what he called the "superficial intimacy" of
the crowd at the beach, "a vulgar and vociferous familiarity so dear to
those prosperous people." The sense of distance is palpable. In Martí's

descriptions, we see an image of Coney Island in the 1880s, but more than that, we sense the presence of a sharp observer. Martí's legacy depends less on the descriptions of a new resort for the masses than on the stance of that observer, on a critical point of view that is still vital, that has survived magnificent iron contraptions, long ago rusted into oblivion. At Coney Island, Martí faced modernity; in other words, he faced the future, our future. He admired progress, and Coney Island, dazzling in miles of electric lights, was its brand new emblem, but he would not take progress at face value.

Like Emerson, Martí recognized a troubling coarseness in the expanding materialism of the United States. He felt that something had shifted in human relations. He wondered if the easy pleasures of a carnival show might not distract from more pressing goals, might not in fact limit or distort human potential. Martí cast a Latin American gaze on the spectacle of Coney Island. It was an original, foundational gaze, combining a sense of distance with a sense of kinship: distance from the din of modernity; kinship with North America's progressive traditions. Martí used his knowledge of Emerson to get a grip on a new landscape and to define what it meant to be a Latin exile in a place that amazed and troubled him. In the distorted mirrors of Coney Island, Martí saw himself anew, and he asked his readers to share that vision. In doing so, he echoed Emerson's advice in "Self-Reliance": in the midst of the crowd, to keep "with perfect sweetness the independence of solitude" (*Essays* 38).

At Coney Island Martí saw the fragments of a culture thrown on the "majestic beach," under the warm, serene sun. Nature became a silent backdrop for an endless parade, impossible to grasp in a single image, impossible to condense in a single sentence, in a paragraph, even in a book. What amazed the visitor was not one detail or another; he was awed rather by the multiplicity of images and sensations hurled at him. What truly amazed was "size, quantity, the sudden results of human activity" ("el tamaño, la cantidad, el resultado súbito de la actividad humana") (9:125).

In Martí's time, machines still dazzled. He wrote with admiration about steamboats, locomotives, carrousels and the complex machinery used to build the Brooklyn Bridge, a marvel of modern engineering completed in 1883. Coney Island had been called a "summer safety valve," but Martí transformed the expression as he translated it into Spanish, calling it "an immense valve of pleasure open to an immense population," a machine literally designed to release the pressures of life in the city through pleasure for the throngs. It was a place where, from a distance, the crowd at a restaurant looked like an army, where roads were not roads but "long carpets covered with human heads." Everything was movement, changing forms, "the feverish rivalry of riches." Everything was monumental, frenetic, incomparable and paradoxical. Martí called it "a crushing expansion" ("esa expansividad anonmadora") (9:125).

In such a place, details faded as everything was pulled into a spinning vortex. What seemed marvelous and unreal to the lone observer had become natural for those in the crowd. Martí wrote of "esa naturalidad en lo maravilloso," (that naturalness in what is marvelous, or fantastic (9:125)). In other words, a fragmented culture, carnival-like in its overwhelming variety, superimposed on nature, the sun, the ocean, the sky, had become reality for thousands of human beings. Martí's vision of Coney Island was also a vision of the metropolis and of the shattered world it had become. In order to grasp it, to understand it and to survive in it, old perceptions and old ways of writing had to be discarded. Through the arcades of the amusement park, ablaze with the new light of thousands of electric bulbs, Martí discovered modernity as a virtual reality, harrowing yet open to creative possibilities.

Martí realized that Coney Island was a huge stage, with thousands of actors, a daily outdoor festival for the people, running from "June to October, from morning until late at night, without interruption, without any change whatsoever." It was a pleasure machine available to rich and poor, to corseted ladies in extravagant hats and gentlemen in frock coats and to the huddled masses yearning to be entertained. At Coney Island "all visible sadness and poverty" were erased, or covered in grease paint. Indeed, money seemed to grow on trees, and even good fortune was for sale. A "hefty German woman" wrote it on a piece of paper, put in an envelope and sold it for fifty cents (9:126).

Alone in the crowd, Martí proposed an antidote to the forlorn sadness he felt in the midst of the rowdy, colorful display of humanity by the beach. He found that antidote in his own version of the contrast between the world of things, evident all around him, and the realm of the spirit. If Coney Island dazzled with its bright lights, it was nonetheless obvious that it was a constructed world, a fleeting chimera that time, changing fashions, fire and the wrecking ball of urban planning would surely destroy. Latin Americans had only limited access to such a world. Once they experienced it, it might be love at first sight, but Martí wanted to offer something more solid and more lasting.

In Martí's "Coney Island," as the glittering outline of piers and hotels fades in the mist, we hear something of his own experience in the United States. Here, he wrote, "a melancholy sadness" takes hold of us. First impressions may have flattered the senses, beguiled the eyes, and clouded reason, yet the anguish of solitude takes over at last. Referring to Latin Americans living in the North, Martí writes that "nostalgia for a superior spiritual world invades them and saddens them . . . because that great land is devoid of spirit" ("la nostalgia de un mundo espiritual superior los invade y aflige . . . porque aquella gran tierra está vacía de espíritu") (9:126).

In his articles on Coney Island, along with the colorful details expected of a travel writer, he relied on sharp contrasts and dichotomies, easily grasped by his readers. Martí admired the pragmatic spirit and ingenuity of the United States. He revered its democratic tradition. Yet he immediately recognized the seductive power of mass culture, already in full swing at Coney Island. He also saw that in the wealthiest of nations, thousands were hungry and sick, literally left out in the cold. Like Riis and other reformers of the period, he had to bear witness, but only Martí wrote for Latin readers, not only those in Latin American but those who had settled in the United States, those who supported his struggle for justice and those who might be persuaded to do so.

In another article on Coney Island, published in October 1883, Martí was more explicitly critical. The hyperboles of the earlier article now approach the grotesque. In one description, a hotel kitchen appears as huge as "the stomach of a monster," feeding a horde as large as an army. From this excremental image, Martí takes us to a Dantesque vision of the city, rendered in an expressionistic style that prefigures the startling contrasts of the surrealists. "Over there in the city, in the tainted barrios, above the rooftops, filthy, bony hands rise up like the ragged flags of a huge, marching army" (allá en la ciudad, en los barrios infectos de donde se ven salir por sobre los techos de las casas, como harapientas banderas de tremendo ejército en camino, mugrientas manos descarnadas) (9:458). The description of urban misery again brings to mind the squalor photographed by Jacob Riis during those same years. It is as if the images captured by Riis are rendered by Martí in a web of human misery:

> There in the damp streets, where men and women are heaped together, writhing . . . without air and without space . . . there in dark, tortuous buildings, where people live in filth and poverty in their stinking rooms, heavy with dark, dank air.
>
> Allá en las calles húmedas donde hombres y mujeres se amasan y revuelven, sin aire y sin espacio . . . allá en los edificios tortuosos y lóbregos donde la gente de hez o de penuria vive en hediondas celdas, cargadas de aire pardo y pantanoso. (9:458)

Summer brought the dreaded cholera, which killed hundreds of children. Like the ogre in the children's fable, cholera sucked the life out of them: "a boa constrictor will not do to children what summer in New York does to poor children" (un boa no los dejará como el verano de New York deja a los niños pobres) (9:458). The city had become an insatiable mechanical monster. Crowded trains ran through its veins, and its maws were a tangle of piers, busy day and night.

The images in Martí's vivid descriptions also recall the horrors painted by Goya. Martí rendered the image of the sick children in a style that was already remarkably modernist: "their eyes are like caves; their skulls, the bald heads of old men; their hands, bunches of dried weeds" (sus ojitos parecen cavernas; sus cráneos, cabezas calvas de hombres viejos; sus manos manojos de yerbas secas). In his second article on Coney Island, Martí's attack on a system that, despite unprecedented wealth, allowed children to die of hunger and disease, is explicit: "I say that this is a public crime, and that it is the duty of the State to remedy such unnecessary misery!" (¡Y digo que éste es un crimen público, y que el deber de remediar la miseria innecesaria es un deber del Estado!) (9:458). Soon after his arrival in the United States, Martí echoed the words of those who were laying the groundwork for twentieth-century activism against the legacy of laissez-faire Social Darwinism. Martí considered that individual misery was not someone else's problem but constituted "a public crime." Like Henry George, author of *Progress and Poverty* (1879), and other reformers he admired, Martí believed that the rise of an economic aristocracy would endanger the rights to which all are entitled in a democratic nation. He called Henry George an advocate for working people and a fighter for the values of a "legitimate democracy." "Many Latin Americans," he wrote for *La Nación*, December 7, 1886, "defend him [Henry George] with their words and their influence" (11:96).

In Martí's writings about Coney Island, the boisterous, outrageous behavior of the crowd frames the lonely figure of a man in black. His intense gaze registers it all, yet he remains invisible. At Coney Island Martí saw two distinct versions of the United States, and he feared that the two would drift apart, with dire consequences to follow. He saw wondrous resources and boundless human energy. He saw a creeping infatuation with the gaudy trappings of prosperity and an alarming rift between rich and poor.

Like Emerson, Martí celebrated the "healthy commerce" between human beings and nature. "Nature" here does not refer only to the uncultivated wilderness but extends to works created by the advance of civilizations: houses, factories and cities. Martí was no provincial romantic, pining for a lost Arcadia. On the contrary, he admired progress, as long as it was planned and orderly, and as long as it benefited the common good. Like Emerson, he believed that human beings derived strength and dignity from "the wide river, the vast sky, the tilled field, the swift railroad, the clean cities." Moreover, he admired the North's tradition of civic activism, evident in the work of abolitionist and reformer Wendell Phillips (1811–1884), whom Martí eulogized as one "consumed by the desire to remedy human misery" (13:58).

In the vacant stare of the poor children of the city, Martí saw the other side of wealth and prosperity. A few good people paid to send a boatload of sick children and their mothers to Coney Island. The children, Martí wrote, "look like broken lilies, pulled up from the mud." But charity would not solve the problem, whose causes, outlined by Martí, are still sadly familiar: lack of education, unemployment, inadequate housing, domestic violence. In a few compact sentences, Martí summarized the economic woes of the period. Domestic overproduction caused an oversupply of manufactured goods. Compounding the problem were prohibitive trade tariffs and competition abroad from cheaper goods. The predictable result: a stagnant economy. As Martí saw it, the United States had two options: Either redefine its priorities and put its house in order or expand and control international markets for "the plethora of products" it produced. Martí hoped for the first solution: a state that would promote the common good and narrow a widening gap between rich and poor. He knew that the second solution, expansion and control of international markets, was already in the works, with Cuba as the perfect stepping stone to Latin America. Martí's fear that the United States would take over Cuba and expand its might throughout Latin America is a recurring topic in his writings, especially in the 1890s. It is a central theme in "Our America," discussed in chapter 4. In a final unfinished letter to his Mexican friend Manuel Mercado, dated May 18, 1895, the day before his death, Martí argues that Cuba's war of independence must prevent "the annexation of Cuba to the United States . . . a hateful, absurd compromise" (20:162).

The spectacle of Coney Island, an immense fair by day, a blaze of lights by night, dazzled the artist in Martí. He gave in to the vision and forced his native language into uncharted regions. Cruising the sparkling canal, like "noble secular gods," he saw "majestic white steamers." What a pleasure not to see, he wrote, an unclean beach, or filthy villages, or somber, abandoned roads. In the mind's eyes, Martí superimposed an image of poverty, reminiscent of conditions he surely witnessed in Cuba and in Latin America, on the sunny shores of Coney Island.

There is more than mere irony in the contrast between a booming Coney Island and a forlorn village in Latin America. Martí's admiration was sincere, but so was his apprehension that there was something rotten underneath the shrill gaiety and the technological brilliance he witnessed. He feared that the boundless energy of the "Colossus of the

North" would crush the spirit, undermine disinterested love between people, discard what could not be put to use or yield a quick profit and ultimately trample the rights of individuals.

Martí's insight did not stop at the dramatic contrast between a materialistic North and a Latin spirit powerless to resist it. This rather simplistic formula became popular throughout Latin America, especially after the publication of *Ariel* (1900), by the Uruguayan writer José Enrique Rodó (1871–1917). Martí's vision is less dualistic. In many of his comments on the United States, Martí is more than merely "anti-American," in the predictable way of a provincial demagogue. His experience of life in New York City and his knowledge of North American culture gave him a keen insight into the ways of the empire. For Martí, the dearth of spirit he witnessed ran counter to a tradition that was in danger of losing its sacred links to individual dignity, respect for nature and mutual love. Love itself was being tagged as a sentimental bibelot, mass produced and sold to the millions, when it should have been the binding force of any society.

For Martí, Coney Island also became an emblem of the shattered landscape of exile. In the funhouse mirrors of the amusement park, he saw a new reflection of himself. In many of his writings, in the introspective moments of his essays and especially in his poetry, there is a fragmented self, an exile whose only home might be the literary realm he has created. After Martí's death on the battlefield, he became a national hero. His stature increased even as the dreams he died for vanished. This is the paradox of his legacy. In death he became an icon. His wisdom, reduced to dazzling epigraphs, was carved in stone. School children declaimed his poems in quaint, annual celebrations of his birthday. Savvy politicos mined his works for clever sound-bites. Yet, away from the trite din of fame, in his writings, something of his original voice still speaks to us today.

In his book, *The Rough Riders*, first published in 1899, Theodore Roosevelt wrote about the war in Cuba as a struggle between North Americans and Spaniards. The Cubans, he wrote, "turned out to be nearly useless" (75), so useless, in fact, that at the signing of the peace treaty between Spain and the United States, there were no Cubans present. The angry protests of Máximo Gómez, the Dominican general who was revered as a leader in Cuba's wars for independence, went unheeded. Cuba, along with Puerto Rico and the Philippines, became part of a new colonial empire. In 1902, Cuba became a lame republic, run by a gaggle of self-serving politicos, who looked to Washington for their next cue. Those who demanded not only independence but true sovereignty and justice, in the spirit of Martí, struggled in a minefield of obstacles.

Yet in Martí's writings there is still a voice that some of us may want to hear. His vision of Coney Island is not merely the jeremiad of a self-righteous observer. It is an insider's critique, a Latin perspective on a brave new world that Martí was beginning to appropriate and to make his own. Like Martí, writers and artists from the United States, from Stephen Crane to Henry Miller to Lou Reed, found in Coney Island a compelling place from which to consider the larger culture and their own position in it. According to John Kasson, in *Amusing the Million*, for American painters in revolt against decorous traditional standards, Coney Island "offered in profusion the ingredients of a powerful new aesthetic" (88). Something of that aesthetic is already evident in Martí's vision of the amusement park as microcosm of the imperial city. Coney Island was the place where the distractions of the crowd served to sharpen the concentration of the lone observer. The ambivalent fascination of Coney Island for early modernist writers and artists prefaces its iconic presence in the poem by mid-century Beat poet Lawrence Ferlinghetti, whose "A Coney Island of the Mind" (1958) reveals an uncanny echo of Martí.

By the time Ferlinghetti wrote his syncopated eulogy, Coney Island was a ramshackle shadow of its former glory, and for that reason all the more appealing to a beat sensibility. "A Coney Island of the Mind" opens with lines that might have been influenced by Martí, although this is probably not the case. Ferlinghetti wrote: "In Goya's greatest scenes we seem to see/ the people of the world/ exactly at the moment when/ they first attainted the title of 'suffering humanity'/ They writhe upon the stage in a veritable rage of adversity" (9). Like Martí's, Ferlinghetti's Coney Island both repels and beguiles. It is a place where the shards of popular cultures are scattered, a place that provokes outrage at the ravages of progress and at the same time seduces in unexpected ways. In other words, the Coney Island of the 1950s became a place to make poetry because it lay on the fringes of mainstream, hopelessly square cultural values, because it allowed the writer to set a venerable American rant against materialism in a new stage and cast it a new language. Coney Island became an ideal setting for portraying the estrangement of modernity, for giving voice to its anguished sense of homelessness, for celebrating fleeting glimpses of its joys. Ferlinghetti wrote of the new hordes of visitors to the park: "They are the same people only further from home/ on freeways fifty lanes wide/ on a concrete continent/ spaced with bland billboards/ illustrating imbecile illusions of happiness" (9).

It is true that in Martí's view of Coney Island there is a strong moral tone and a sense of distance, but his stance is not all of a piece. He took pleasure in the sight of two young lovers "under a red umbrella, leaning on their elbows," oblivious to the world around them. Unlike Rodó, whose praise of the Latin spirit is numbingly incorporeal, Martí always returns to the body, those that surround him and his own. His call to the life of the spirit does not lead to a radical separation from the body. In Martí, appeals to the spirit, so dear to nineteenth-century sensibilities, are weighed with a return to the things of the body. Throughout his works, in prose and in poetry, the return to the body defines a compelling pattern, one that has projected Martí into our own present, far from the starched pronouncements of musty ideologues of the spirit. In one of his difficult *Versos libres*, the body is wracked and devoured: "The mother of all pain I keep in my bones . . . Not a single pore without a wound" ("La madre del dolor guardo en mis huesos . . . Ni un poro sin herida") (16:222). "In his poetry, the body of the poem is a body open to pain, to life, to the other. It is a body that looks for the body of the other" (Ette, in *Re-reading Martí* 50).

In his essays on Coney Island, Martí combined the high moral tone of the prophet crying in the wilderness with a gaze informed by the presence and the call of the body. Martí's ambivalence toward the culture of progress is not unique. In his writings on the United States, there are echoes of Emerson and foreshadowings of the dissonant strains of twentieth-century writers. There is also in Martí a prelude to "The poet's eye obscenely seeing" of Ferlinghetti's Coney Island (13) and to Andrew Delbanco's contemporary jeremiad, *The Real American Dream*. There is in Martí a novel view of the fragmented nature of modern culture, of its power to hide misery under deceiving masks, as in Ferlinghetti's "all the other fatal shorn-up fragments/ of the immigrant's dream come too true/ and mislaid/ among the sunbathers" (13).

Martí's Latin version of this "mislaying" of the dream is seminal and unique. Martí wrote that Coney Island was a "valve of pleasure," open at full throttle and not easily turned off. He suggested a Latin difference that might be its antidote. His inclusive "we" is not an editorial convention or a supercilious gesture of identity. It is the pronoun of radical democracy and refers to "other nations, we among them." It refers to people everywhere whose history and whose values give them pause before the easy glee and uneven prosperity of the United States, the only nation, Martí wrote, that "has the absolute duty to be great" (la nación única que tiene el deber absoluto de ser grande) (9:27).

We live, Martí wrote, "devoured by a sublime inner demon," a desire for love and glory that once attained, becomes a new goal, a new ambition. The eagle, once seized, Martí wrote in a characteristic metaphor, is transformed into a rebellious butterfly, which dares us to follow it and chains us to its intricate flight. He was referring to a creative spirit that might drive some to artistic creation and others to action, or to both, as it happened with him. Martí's own desires took him from his books to the battlefield. For other Latinos and Latinas, he wanted something more than "the immigrant's dream come too true/ and mislaid/ among the sunbathers" (Ferlinghetti 13). Yet his call to the things of the spirit is not limited to Latin people, "*la gente latina*" as Martí called us. Martí's is an expansive call beyond the boundaries of narrow, parochial nationalisms. He felt that the people of the United States also needed to change, for "despite appearances they are merely united by interests, and by the polite mutual hatred of those who haggle over the same goal." Martí felt that the need for change, change for "something more lasting," was imperative. "It is indispensable to create a common atmosphere for isolated spirits. It is indispensable to feed the light and starve the beast" (Es indispensable crear a los espíritus aislados una atmósfera común. Es indispensable alimentar la luz, y achicar la bestia) (10:375).

Martí felt that citizenship in any republic meant not only guarantee of individual rights but a shared sense of civility, in the broadest sense of the term. Without civic duties, which translate into responsibility for the common good, citizenship is a wasted privilege. Feed the light or feed the beast, that is Martí's message. The light is wisdom and freedom, or rather wisdom in freedom: For Martí, freedom did not simply mean the right of each individual to do as he or she pleased. Without a sense of the common good, freedom turns into the fleeting satisfaction of selfish pleasures. Without the desire to guarantee the privilege for everyone, freedom is not worthy of its name. That desire is what Martí called "the light"; the beast was everything that opposed it.

In the Coney Island of 1883, and in the vast country that surrounded it, the beast was everywhere, but so was the light. Martí, our first poet in New York, saw it clearly, "the spectacle of luxury, the desire to possess it," and the need to get beyond it. Success in the world is a worthy goal, but it need not banish "contact with great ideas and noble acts," and with "the knowledge of the harmony of the universe" (10:376). This is not the lament of a belated prophet or the preaching of an ascetic idealist. For "*Nuestra América*," he wanted prosperity and the freedom to act responsibly, and the possibility of some "commerce with the stars."

CHAPTER 2

THE NEW WOMAN AND THE ANXIETIES OF GENDER

In Martí's *Versos sencillos* (simple verses), "Eva is false." Eva, the emblematic name given to a female character in the poems, is alternately treacherous and consoling. Like her famous Biblical namesake, Eva, the iconic woman, cannot tell the difference between a real jewel and a fake, between truth and deceit, or in the context of the poems, between the real love of a man and its counterfeit. In the poems, a male subject desires and mistrusts an image of woman whose representation he paradoxically controls. From these not at all original observations, one may proceed to a predictable and familiar reading of the poems, in which all female characters are reflected in an omnipotent male gaze. Such a reading, though certainly viable, would not account for Martí's ambiguous positions regarding not only women but also gender differences and the qualities that were attached to them in the late nineteenth century. In other words, examples of Martí's "narrow vision of rigid gender roles" (Hewitt 32n) are plentiful and rather predictable. On the other hand, it will be more useful to consider some of the uses of gender differences in Martí's writings, to account for both the specific resonance of familiar clichés regarding women's "faults" and the points at which the radical gender binaries of the period shift in suggestive ways. The point then is not to review Martí's obvious machismo but to look more closely as his rhetoric of gender, especially in light of the changing role of women in the United States during his New York years, 1880–1895.

Throughout his works, Martí uses gender-based metaphors and imagery to define key concepts and to advance fundamental arguments. Nationalism, Americanism, noble sacrifice, the triumphs of the spirit, a cosmic vision centered on "man's" infinitely renewable potential: These are the pillars of what generations of Spanish-speaking readers have called *el ideario martiano*, not Martí's "ideology" but rather a more loosely defined "body of principles." Gender differences and the symbolic language that such differences generate should be read alongside the more familiar and more prestigious topics of Martí's *ideario*.

Many readers have noted that the tension between virility and femininity frequently marks and at times determines the style in which Martí's strong body of principles has been presented. The rhetoric of gender differences informs much of what Martí has to say about the tension between the pleasures of the senses and the imperatives of moral rectitude, between the privacy of the erotic and the virile duties of the public sphere. Martí can be guarded, distant and self-contained, most famously perhaps in "Coney Island." Standing on the crowded beach, his "I" is not Whitman's multitudinous, all-embracing entity. On the other hand, on the eve of his death, in the *Diaries*, there is a joyous embrace of all others—the bookseller, the ragged peasant, the fetching young woman, the splendid young man. The tensions and anxieties associated with gender differences define an erratic, circuitous trajectory, which prefaces the final glimpse of a different vision, and perhaps a different order of things in the *War Diaries*.

If woman's "frailty" is a recurring topic, there is also the self-sacrificing heroic woman, epitomized by Mariana Grajales, the formidable matriarch of the Maceos. The editors of Martí's *Obras completas* (complete works) have placed "the Mother of the Maceos," a legendary figure in Cuba, at the heart of a section simply titled "Women," in which maternity, valor and self-sacrifice are praised as supreme values. These conventional, often highly sentimentalized images of woman offer a sharp contrast to Martí's comments on working women and the "woman movement," as it was then called. Dispersed throughout his works, these comments are thoughtful and provocative, even when they remain ambiguously grounded on the very polarities that the women's movement sought to undermine.

The ambiguity is not Martí's alone, but rather it is characteristic of proto-feminism in the closing years of the nineteenth century. In *The Grounding of Modern Feminism*, Nancy F. Cott writes of a "tactical" duality in the early struggle for woman's equality. Early leaders in this struggle wanted women to be the equal of men, yet they often insisted on the unique, that is, gender-specific contributions of women to the republic. Something of this "functional ambiguity," Cott's term, is apparent in many of Martí's comments on women.

If at times Martí seems hopelessly nineteenth-century in his representation of an idealized femininity, at other times his comments rattle the established molds of his time. It is easy enough to say that Martí's view of women and his conventional acceptance of established gender roles are a product of his time. It is more difficult to unravel from his writings those instances that suggest a more progressive view, which includes an understanding of the inevitable evolution of women's roles, even when those changes exacerbated the personal anxieties of a male, heterosexual subject.

In Martí's anxieties regarding changes in the social, cultural and political status of women, there is also the intuition of radical shifts in the future roles of gender. Martí does not explicitly articulate the implications of this shift, but signs of such a shift are present in some of his writings, especially in his use of gender-based metaphors. In the poems, there is the "false Eve," a dangerous temptress. By contrast, in his notes, there is a critical reading of the biblical tale of Adam and Eve, which he rejects in favor of a Native American version of the creation myth, in which all creatures issue from a single "seed." In another entry in his notebooks, Martí criticizes traditional marriage and advocates for a partnership of equals. I will return to these passages.

In a chronicle about life in New York, published two years after his arrival in the city, Martí discusses the women's movement and praises the powerful oratory of one of the women at the closing of a meeting in support of female suffrage. Martí's comments on the women's movement are included in one of the many articles on New York City that he sent to *La Opinión Nacional* in Caracas, Venezuela. In his article, published on February 18, 1882, Martí touches on a series of events under the topic of "life and death in the city." However, despite the variety of topics covered in some of these articles, the rather abrupt transitions from one topic to the next harmonize in the end in a series of suggestive juxtapositions. In this 1882 article, Martí covers the following topics: the many seasonal dances in the city, a catastrophic fire, the condition of working women, and lastly, a compact summary of the developing agenda of the women's movement.

In his article for *La Opinión Nacional*, Martí writes about the winter social season in New York City, which included a series of formal soirées and costume balls attended by hundreds of well-heeled New Yorkers and those aspiring to that status. The dances given by New York's French community, whose members "numbered in the thousands," were especially "exuberant in color and joy." While winter gripped the city, the elegant dances offered a stunning display of luxury and "conspicuous consumption," a term that Martí might have readily embraced, although it was coined by Thorstein Veblen in his *Theory of the Leisure Class*, first published in 1899. "Magnificent carriages . . . wait in front of the opulent Academy of Music," Martí writes, where "elegant ladies display their dazzling jewels" (9:245). In the midst of luxury and pomp, Martí introduces a scene worthy of a photograph by Jacob Riis:

Angry and blaspheming, the most despicable or most unfortunate men in the city crowd at the narrow doors of miserable lodging houses, in whose nauseating rooms, drunk with liquor and with hatred, which is as intoxicating as liquor, hundreds of boarders lie naked on the floor, around an ancient red-hot stove.

AglomÉranse, colÉricos y blasfemantes, los hombres mÁs ruines o los mÁs desventurados de la ciudad, a las puertas estrechas de miserables casas de dormir, en cuyas alcobas nauseabundas, ebrios de licor y de odio, que embriaga como el licor, yacen desnudos por el suelo, en torno a una vieja estufa enrojecida, centenares de huéspedes. (9:244-245)

At the French dance, a costume ball, "[r]ough warriors, in armor and gauntlets, dance with courting pages, who look like blushing goblets, brimming with Burgundy wine" (Danzan guerreros duros, armados de coraza y guanteletes, con pajecillos enamoradores, que parecen tazas sonrosadas, rebosantes de espumoso vino de Borgoña) (9:245). Martí is referring to couples in costume: the men as knights and the women cross-dressing as their adoring pages. The dance is visually rich, and Martí takes evident delight in describing it. Yet pleasure is tempered with an implicit mistrust of artifice and deceit, associated with wealthy women, corseted, feathered, bejeweled and even cross-dressed in the extravagant styles of the period. In the dances Martí describes, men can also be false, especially when they lack virile qualities, as in the case of "a painted viscount, keeping time on a tambourine," one of the characters in another costume ball presented in one of his poems: "Marca un vizconde pintado/ El tiempo en la pandereta" (16:97).

In the blink of an eye, Martí takes his reader from the opulent dances of the 1882 winter season to a raging fire in another part of the city: "It has been a terrible spectacle, whose presence did not disturb the cheer of the lovers of the dance" (Ha sido un espectáculo terrible, cuya presencia no alcanzó a turbar el regocijo de los enamorados de la danza) (9:246). Now it is the flames that dance, raging through a building full of printing shops. Like a seasoned reporter, Martí takes his readers from scenes of opulence to the sight of utter devastation, from fashion to social commentary, from admiration for a woman's dazzling gown to an earnest critique of a system that condemns women and men to poverty and hunger.

Early in the freezing morning, even as the last partygoers were heading home in their fancy carriages, a building housing the printing shops of the most important newspapers in the city burst into flames. The *Sun*, the *Tribune*, the *World* and the *Times* ("an austere daily whose young editor is honest and blunt"), all had part of their printing operations in the burning building. "The upper floors, full of workers, poor young

women who work as typesetters, and messenger boys, were full of horror and screams" (Los pisos altos, llenos de trabajadores, de pobres
mozas, que hacen oficio de cajistas, de niños recaderos, se llenaron de
horror y de clamores) (9:246). Martí now focuses on the plight of the
women trapped in the upper floors, their flowing skirts an easy prey to a
"beast" of fire. He underscores the appalling working conditions of
women, now trapped on the upper floors, where the firemen's ladders
could not reach them:

> You can see a poor black woman, who, as if chased by ferocious mon-
> sters, jumps screaming out of a burning room. She cowers on the ledge of
> a window, holds on with her burning hand so as not to plunge to the
> street, and suddenly stands upright, gathers her skirt between her legs, lets
> out a horrendous scream, and jumps to the street. Her body, crashing
> against the pavement, is mangled with a loud noise.
>
> Vese a una pobre negra, que, como perseguida de monstruos feroces,
> salta dando hondos gritos de un cuarto encendido, se acurruca en el
> umbral de una ventana, se ase por no caer a la calle, de su mano ardiente,
> y se yergue de súbito, se recoge las ropas entre ambas piernas, exhala
> un alarido, y se arroja a la calle, en cuyas piedras chocó su cuerpo,
> despedazado con estruendo. (9:246–247)

The horror of this woman's death is highlighted by the pathos of her
final gesture, gathering her voluminous skirts between her legs before
plunging to her death. In another scene, "a heroic Negro" climbs a pole
to cut a telegraph wire, attached to the burning building at its other end;
three men then use the severed cable to climb down to safety. A young
woman, her hands stained with typesetting ink, tears off pieces of her
burning dress, jumps to the top of a ladder and into the arms of a fire-
man. Another woman, "as if dressed in flames," plunges back into the
building, "seized by the hungry beast." "Today everything is ashes. All
that remains is respect for the brave, who have been honored with
medals." The analogy between the passion and opulence of the dance
and the flames, which dance and "clothe" their victims, is sustained
throughout (9:247).
    From a description of the ruins of the building Martí moves on to a
compact summary of the situation of working women, which in turn
prefaces a commentary on the women's movement. The apocalyptic scenario of the burning building prefaces the no less radical changes associated with the women's movement. As he does in other essays, Martí
suggests that in difficult times, radical changes may emerge from old
ruins. This fire and many others like it killed scores of working people,
many of them young women. In his description of the charred ruins and

in his comments on the fate of those who worked there, Martí suggests that the women's movement in the United States is best understood in light of the deplorable situation of working people:

> In those ruins [of the burned-out building] one can see, like warriors in a good fight, dead in the midst of battle, the frames that held the typesetting cases, operated by frail women in exchange for a miserable salary. In these hazy mornings that look more like early dawn, it is true that it fills one with sorrow to see, coming in from distant suburbs, these brave [female] workers, who returning home the previous evening after a day of hard work, laid their restless heads, without time to dream, on a cold, hard pillow.
>
> En esos escombros asoman, como guerreros de buena batalla, muertos en la mitad de guerrear, las armazones que sustentaban las cajas de tipos de imprimir, manejados a cambio de ruin salario, por débiles mujeres. Es verdad que llena de dolor ver venir de lejanos suburbios, en estas mañanas turbias que parecen madrugadas, a esas obreras valerosas que, al volver en la noche anterior de su ruda faena, reclinaron la inquieta cabeza, sin tiempo de soñar, en su almohada dura y fría. (9:247–8)

Martí is awed by the sheer number of women in the workforce of New York City. The women crowd into ferries and buses, looking like hordes of orphans, their cheeks faded, their hands swollen: "Male workers are protected by thick overcoats, while the women wear faded, thin, ragged dresses. They work like a man and earn a miserable wage, much lower than that of a man" (Van los obreros amparados de trajes gruesos, y ellas, de telas descoloridas, delgadas y ruines. Hacen la labor de un hombre, y ganan un jornal mezquino, much más bajo que el de un hombre) (9:248). Martí takes his readers from a dance where women's role is to serve as mannequins for dresses and jewels, to a fire where working men and women die, to the situation of working women, and finally to the efforts of the women's movement to "remedy such misery, which destroys body and soul" (9:248).

If the image of women fighting for their rights was radical in New York at the end of the nineteenth century, it was surely scandalous for many of Martí's readers in Latin America. As if to placate those reader, Martí prefaces his sympathetic summary of the women's movement with a contrast between an idealized image of Latin American women, frail and delicate, and the militant, working women of the northern metropolis. The contrast plays into the prejudices of Martí's male and female readers in Latin America and certainly suggests that Martí himself shares the premise of such prejudices. On the other hand, Martí's comments are also a tactical bridge between the changing role of women in an industrialized society and the more traditional view of woman as sub-servient lover and devoted homemaker, dear to many of Martí's readers in Latin America:

> There is in this land [the United States] a group of women, who work with vivacity and intelligence for the achievement of the reforms to which they aspire. Except for the fact that manly women do not please our poetic, noble race, these innovators would seem worthy of the reforms for which they struggle.
>
> Hay en esta tierra un grupo de mujeres, que batallan con una vivacidad y un ingenio tales en el logro de reformas a que aspiran, que, a no ser porque no placen mujeres varoniles a nuestra raza poética e hidalga, parecerían estas innovadoras dignas de las reformas por que luchan. (9:248)

Martí identifies with those readers who cherish the role of women as either frail virgins or fecund housewives; yet he presents the new role of women in a northern metropolis as the product of specific social circumstances, in order to suggest that the new woman and her struggle for equality should not be judged using our Latin preconceptions. Martí writes that Latin men, himself included, see women as "frail" or "full of life." In Martí's fraternal "we" (men), women fulfill a stereotype of purity, "guarded with tenderness and care" by a loving family. Class and, more subtly, racial stereotypes, play into Martí's image of an idealized, and oddly distanced, Latin woman: "That elegant lily [*Aquel lirio elegante*] that perfumes our balconies, as it does our soul." By contrast, a man in the North sees in woman "a partner in battle [*una compañera de batalla*], of whom he demands strong arms for the struggle" (9:248).

Martí's brief but sharp discussion of the women's movement in 1882 is framed by the contrast between wealth and poverty in the city, a contrast dramatized by the fire that sent working men and women plunging to their deaths. In this context, the women's struggle is entirely justified, even if it shocks Latin readers in Caracas or Buenos Aires. Martí seems to pacify his Latin readers by sharing their anxiety over what to them may be the "vulgar and extravagant" behavior of the women who speak out for their rights. At the same time, he insists that their demands are "legitimate," the term he uses, given the dire circumstances he has just described.

Martí underscores the seriousness and high-mindedness of the women's congress and quotes from one of the speeches, pronounced by "a respectable old lady, with such rich diction and such proper gestures, that there was no room for ridicule, so that friends and adversaries listened attentively and clapped their hands." Evidently addressing men as the oppressors of women, the woman quoted by Martí has this to say:

The only way of life that you allow us is is to be a servant or a hypocrite! If we are rich, you deplete our inheritance! If we are poor, you pay us a miserable wage! If we are single, you desire us like fragile toys! If we are married, you deceive us brutally! You flee after you pervert us because we are perverted! Since you leave us alone, then give us the means to live alone. Give us the vote, so that we can give ourselves these means.

¡No nos dejáis más modo de vivir que ser siervas, o ser hipócritas! ¡Si ricas, absorbéis nuestras herencias! ¡Si pobres, nos dais un salario miserable! ¡Si solteras, nos anheláis como a juguetes quebradizos! ¡Si casadas, nos burláis brutalmente! ¡Nos huís, luego que nos pervertís, porque estamos pervertidas! Puesto que nos dejáis solas, dadnos los medios de vivir solas. Dadnos el sufragio, para que nos demos estos medios.' (9:249)

Although Martí qualifies his own position and seems to soothe the ego of his male readers by sharing the stereotype of woman as virgin and mother, he quotes from the woman's speech with evident admiration and without judgment. In Martí's poetry and prose, a marginal, dangerous woman, "perverted" by the city, threatens the "virility" of the poet. The relationship between Martí's Latin stereotypes of woman and this degraded feminine image is evident. What is less obvious, but certainly worth considering, is the echo of the feminist critique of woman, degraded by the treatment of men, in Martí's recurring images of a degraded, degrading woman, which may now be regarded not as the exclusive product of Martí's male chauvinism but as the recognition of a type determined by specific social circumstances.

In the speech quoted by Martí, the woman says, "ignorant women, thanks to the helplessness in which they live, become fruits of the night [*frutas de noche*], and guests of the police, and at the police station there are no honest women who might help these unfortunate ones, but rather men who mock them and abuse them! Put women in police stations where women are arrested! Let us vote, and we will put them there!" (9:249).

The image of the prostitute as a "fruit of the night" used by the speaker at the women's congress appears in Martí's articles and most dramatically in one of his *Versos libres* (free verses), in a poem entitled "Love in the City." In the poem, love in the city is fast and ruthless, and a woman becomes a "brimming glass," quickly downed and, once dirtied, easily discarded. Prostitution is not just the way that a destitute woman survives; the industrialist's wife is also a prized possession, as valuable as "a golden bowl or a sumptuous painting" (16:171). The poet's moral integrity and virility are threatened by this degraded woman. In the poems, and in some of the articles and essays, the willful omnipotence of Martí's male gaze is obvious, but a different reading may be suggested in his appropriation of contemporary feminist images of woman as degraded not by a feminine essence but by specific social, political circumstances, which are not only open to criticism but subject to change. In other words, being a rich man's "golden bowl," that is, trading beauty and youth for comfort and security, is not an essential "fault" of woman. In Martí's New York it was an option for comely, young white women, in many cases nurtured from birth for a role as a "luxurious toy" (*un juguete de lujo*) (10:375). It was certainly not an option for the women who worked as typesetters in the burning building, and Martí makes the distinction explicit.

In another abrupt yet telling transition, Martí concludes his article on the women's movement with a brief comment on the way promiment New Yorkers have denounced the persecution of Jews in Russia: "The hearts of the men and women of the earth," he writes, "respond to the cry of anguish of the men and women of Moses" (9:250). This is a rare occasion in which Martí writes of "men and women" not merely of "men" as representatives of all humankind. It is significant that he would do so in an article that also covers a meeting for women's rights. In other contexts, Martí continues to use "men" to refer to all people.

Indeed, Martí follows a recognizable pattern in considering "manliness" as a required characteristic of a worthy male citizen. In the past 20 years or so, scores of studies have considered the complex links between nationalism and sexuality, and more specifically the way that the power and centrality of a national male subject is paradoxically guaranteed by those it confines to various margins, notably women, homosexuals and other "deviants." In a pioneering study, *Nationalism and Sexuality*, George L. Mosse has studied the sources, the implementation and the deviations from a radically dualistic conception of human behavior in the realm of gender and sexuality. An overview of the topic in the works of Martí would certainly place him among those who upheld clear distinction between masculinity and femininity in the making of the nation. At the same time, a closer look at Martí confirms a recurring ambiguity regarding the relationship between nationalism and gender differences.

It should come as no surprise that Martí would condemn effeminacy in men and manliness in women as symptoms of a malaise endemic to large cities. However, as critic Emilio Bejel suggests, Martí's position becomes more ambiguous, and therefore much richer and more suggestive, when he must defend Cuban men when they are branded as effeminate weaklings, unworthy of becoming the colonial subjects of the United States.

On March 6, 1889, the *Manufacturer*, a Philadelphia newspaper, published an article titled "Do We Want Cuba?" The article restates the terms of an old debate regarding the possible annexation of Cuba to the United States, a topic almost as old as the American nation itself. According to the article, Cubans have been incapable of ridding themselves of Spanish rule because they lacked the manly strength to do so. In other words, the most glaring defects of the Cuban "race" are its effeminacy and lack of virile strength. Whatever economic benefits the United States might derive from annexing Cuba, the argument goes, would not justify the Herculean task of ruling a population completely incapable of functioning as virile citizens of a republic. The article easily slips from qualities defined by gender to "race," adding that "Cuban Negroes . . . are clearly at the level of barbarity." "Our only hope of qualifying Cuba for the dignity of statehood," the article concludes, "would be to Americanize her completely, populating her with people of our own race." Yet there is a danger in such a solution, the article concludes, since even "our race," presumably so-called Anglo-Saxons, might "degenerate" under Cuba's tropical sun.

The arguments in the *Manufacturer*'s article are complacently grounded on commonly held notions about the relationship among geography, race and gender characteristics. In the second half of the nineteenth century, a widely accepted proto-fascist discourse was often structured along a northern/southern axis, with the forces of "civilization" concentrated in northern latitudes. As inflexible as it was in its prejudices, the formula was highly adaptable to specific circumstances and could be used to condemn Cubans as well as Africans, Italians or Jews. As shown in chapter three, in his writings on race Martí questioned the very notion of "race" and the making of what he called "bookstore races," that is, manufactured categories designed to separate and oppress people.

Martí's progressive stance went against the grain of the accepted beliefs of his day and in fact prefigures contemporary ideas about race as a constructed category, ambiguously supported by evident differences in the diverse physiognomy of human beings. Obviously neither Martí nor his contemporaries had come to a similar conclusion regarding the construction of gender categories. In Western cultures, the possibility of a range of differences, rather than an inviolate binary, between men and women was, and in some quarters still is, a radical proposition. Yet, faced with the insults hurled by the *Manufacturer*, Martí's defended Cuban manhood "in a quite oblique and evasive manner," as Bejel puts it.

In his defense of Cuban manhood, Martí's arguments suggest that the various characteristics associated with different genders may not be rigidly bound to a "male" or a "female" body. In other words, in a modern nation, a worthy male citizen may incorporate certain "feminine" qualities, such as a gentle, compassionate manner and an appreciation for art and things of the spirit. At the same time, Martí's guarded admiration for the female orators who defended the rights of women suggests that in certain circumstances, some women may adopt some of the qualities associated with men. Martí's position is part of a foundational discourse through which men became leaders of nation not by embracing a radically macho stance but rather by assimilating certain worthy qualities traditionally associated with women. This "secure knot of sentimentalized men," as Doris Sommer writes in her *Foundational Fictions*, became the leaders of the nations of Latin America, which paradoxically excluded women from positions of leadership, consigning them to a series of familiar supporting roles.

In Martí's response to the *Manufacturer*, one might expect a vehement denial of the accusation of "effeminacy" and an affirmation of manliness; on the contrary, Martí's strategy takes a different route, indicative of his own position regarding the *Manufacturer*'s gender-based attack on Cubans and gender differences in general. In his defense of Cuban people, Martí opts for a series of rhetorical questions and implicit negations. Even men of "delicate physique," he argues, and even those who write delicate poetry, have also shown courage in the struggle against a powerful enemy, namely the Spanish government. Thus femininity, if it means a delicate physique and a penchant for poetry, need not be an objectionable quality in a male. In fact, a feminine demeanor may mask the strength to destroy an enemy: If "hiding under the glove that polishes the poem [is] the hand that fells the foe— are we to be considered as the *Manufacturer* does consider us, an 'effeminate' people?" ([Si] ocultando bajo el guante que pule el verso, [está] la mano que derriba al enemigo, ¿se nos ha de llamar, como the *Manufacturer* nos llama, un pueblo 'afeminado'?) (1:238).

"These 'effeminate' Cubans," Martí goes on, "had once courage enough, in the face of a hostile government, to wear on their left arms, for a whole week, the mourning-band for Lincoln." Instead of rejecting the insult, that Cubans are "effeminate," Martí identifies with those same Cubans, while inverting the sense of the offending term. In an article written in November 1889, a few months after the *Manufacturer*'s attack, Martí proudly refers to the fact that some young Cubans, himself among them, dared to wear mourning upon hearing that President Lincoln had been assassinated in 1865. These "fervent boys and enthusiastic virgins," Martí writes, "in their passion for liberty, proudly wore mourning for Lincoln, without fearing Madrid's lieutenants" (6:48). In a later reference to the same event, he writes of "our love for Lincoln for whom we Cubans wore mourning" (3:48). Martí was 12 years old at the time of Lincoln's assassination and his youthful affront to "Madrid's lieutenants." By the time he was 16, he had been condemned to six years of hard labor; he served six months before his family succeeded in obtaining a pardon. The following year, 1871, he was exiled to Spain, his health and his political views forever marked by the horrors of prison.

In another essay on a dance, "A Great Dance in New York," Martí describes a parade of fancy dresses. It was published in April 1888, about a year before the *Manufacturer*'s attack on "effeminate" Cubans. In this same essay, Martí sets the pejorative term "*afeminamiento*" (effeminacy) in the context of a comment about the city's insufficiently "*femenil*" (having feminine qualities) architecture. Here "*femenil*" suggests positive qualities:

> North American man, who barely begins to show signs of effeminacy in the sons of rich people, reflects in his architecture the predominance of his virile habits, and to this day does not reveal in his buildings that feminine grace, that is, balance and taste in life, which does not exert its regulating influence or perhaps might never exert it on national life.
>
> El norteamericano, que apenas empieza a dar en los hijos de sus ricos muestras de afeminamiento, refleja en su arquitectura el predominio de sus hábitos viriles, y no revela hasta hoy en sus edificios aquella gracia feme- nil, nivel y gusto de la vida, que todavía no ha ejercido su influjo regulador ni lo ejercererá nunca acaso, sobre la existencia nacional. (11:393)

In other words, good architecture has a feminine, that is, a graceful quality, absent in the manly buildings of the city, although signs of "effeminacy," that is a softer, more artistic nature, are evident in some of the young men of the privileged class. The term "effeminacy" retains some of its negative charge when applied to the young sons of rich families, yet the immediate use of "feminine" to refer to graceful architecture suggests an admirable quality, which may or may not exert its "regulating influence" on "national life." In certain contexts, Martí rejects the "effeminate man," as Bejel clearly argues, but in others, he uses "effeminacy" and its derivatives to suggest positive qualities, moral and artistic traits that he shares. Moreover, femininity may be synony- mous with "balance and taste," qualities that may be shared by all gen- ders and that indeed provide a "regulating influence" in the life of a nation.

These arguments in favor of feminine qualities that might temper the excesses of a virile nation recall the "functional ambiguity" of the women's movement itself during the years Martí lived in New York City. While insisting on social and political equality, defenders of women's rights at the end of the nineteenth century argued that women's role in the republic would also "counteract the excess of masculinity that is everywhere to be found in our unjust and unequal laws." These are the words of Jane Frohock, a contemporary of Stanton's, quoted by Cott in *The Grounding of Modern Feminism* (19). The terms of the argument are similar to Martí's own when he argues that "femininity" may act as a "regulating influence" on the boundless "virility" of the nation.

It has already been mentioned that, in most of his writings, Martí reproduces the conventional division of labor between men and women, which contrasts them according to their moral and physical qualities and assigns them specific and predetermined roles in society. In the children's magazine he wrote and edited, *La Edad de Oro* (the golden age), "a boy is born to be a gentlemen" and "a girl to be a mother." The girls should learn "pretty stories to entertain their guests" and should "play with their dolls." Boys should learn "what they must know to be real men" (18:301). The magazine was forced to shut down after four issues when its Brazilian backer withdrew his support because he felt that Martí did not include enough material on religion. In a letter to his Mexican friend Mercado, Martí complains that his backer wanted him to constantly mention "the fear of God" instead of "tolerance and the divine spirit." In the same letter, Martí explains that he refused to promote "religious intransigence," which had caused so much suffering already (Toledo Sande 191). In New York, Martí struggled to provide for himself and his family, even as his work for the liberation of Cuba became increasingly demanding. As a successful magazine for children, *La Edad de Oro* might have provided a welcome source of income. However, in this and other such occasions, Martí was unwilling to submit to the censorship of imperious editors or backers; consequently, the magazine folded.

The images of the "boy-gentlemen" and "the girl-wife-mother" in the magazine are representative not only of the dogma of the period but also of Martí's own conception of gender polarities. Given the context of its publication, an impatient backer and an audience of children, parents and teachers, it is no surprise that *La Edad de Oro* is unequivocal in the gender-defined roles assigned to its young readers. Despite the weight of conventional gender roles in Martí's writing, there are nonetheless instances of remarkable flexibility, ambiguity and anxiety on the limits of gender polarities, particularly as a source of imagery to frame and understand the human condition. In Martí, Eve, or Adam for that matter, will not have the last word.

In an article written by Martí in defense of certain poets, published in *Revista Venezolana* (Venezuelan magazine), the radical division of labor between genders gives way to a more ambiguous use of gender qualities to refer to different types of poetic language. In a defense of contemporary male poets accused of being too precious, and implicitly too "feminine," Martí explains that different uses of languages demand different styles, which may have feminine or masculine characteristics, as the case might be. Writing about intimate things requires one type of language; writing about public things requires another. Martí maintains a strict opposition between private and public spaces, whose respective activities are given gender-derived qualities. The style of the interior is soft and gentle, and implicitly feminine, while a public style must be rough and "choleric," that is, manly. However, both "styles" may thrive in the same man:

> There is the language of the private chamber, and that of the rousing speech. One language speaks the harsh debate; another, the peaceful biography. Different pleasures are produced in us, and different styles are required, by the joy, akin to contemplating the setting sun, that comes from a careful contemplation of the past; and the joy, akin to seeing the dawn, of penetrating, anxious and trembling, into the future . . . On the one hand, the necessary conditions are repose, patience; on the other, energy and longing. For that reason the same man may speak different languages when he turns his piercing eyes towards the dead past and when, with the anguish and the ire of the soldier in battle, he wields a new weapon in the choleric battle of the present. (7:211)

In other words, writing about the past requires a sedate, subjective, implicitly feminine style, "the language of the chamber," while writing about the present and the future, which, significantly, Martí fuses into one, requires force and virility, literally, "penetration." Clearly Martí is describing his own experiences as a (male) writer who incorporates both masculine and feminine qualities in order to be a better writer, and a better man. At the same time, Martí recognized that there was no stronger harbinger of the future than the changing role of women in the city and in the unprecedented work of the advocates for the rights of women. In a book entitled *La mujer en Martí* (women in Martí), Onilda Jiménez writes that "Martí could not hide his admiration before the dynamism of women in politics and in their struggle to obtain the right to vote" (129).

In the 1880s their political struggle took many women to the podium at various congresses, still a radical position for a woman. During Martí's years in New York, women who spoke publicly in defense of their rights, along with working women, were transgressing the gender-defined boundaries between private and public spaces. Martí's anxiety before what many were calling "the spectacle" of these women is palpable. At the same time, he acknowledges their power as orators in a field that had belonged exclusively to men, even as he reassures his Latin readers with conventional images of devoted mothers and chaste virgins. Martí seems to be approaching a recognition, unheard of among most men of his generation, certainly among Latin men, of a radical change in the role of women, and consequently in the cultural uses of gender.

Martí does not dismiss the early feminists as "virile" intruders, a common tactic. In 1912, Rubén Darío, a leading *modernista* poet and Martí's contemporary, wrote derisively of feminist women. In fact, Darío coins a term to describe them: "*marivarones*," a "softer variant," he writes, of a vulgar term, obviously "*marimachos*." Both terms may be colloquially though quite accurately translated as "butch women," today a badge of honor for my friend and neighbor but a vulgar insult in Darío's mouth. Whatever the term used to denigrate them, Darío asserts that "*feministas*," the term he uses, "deserve to be punished" (merecen el escarmiento) (2:550). By contrast, Martí writes that one of the speakers at the women's congress is a venerable old woman, in other words, safely beyond the category of temptress or fecund mother. The woman's age puts her beyond the common stereotypes of young female beauty; at the same time, it forces the audience to look beyond appearances and listen to her powerful speech. Gender differences seem to recede, however briefly. Martí writes, "that there was no room for ridicule, [and] that friends and adversaries listened attentively and clapped their hands" (9:249).

Ridicule was indeed the general response to women who spoke out in favor of change and reform regarding their role in society. According to Gail Bederman, author of *Manliness and Civilization*, "men reacted passionately by ridiculing these New Women, prophesying that they would make themselves ill and destroy national life, insisting that they were rebelling against nature" (14). In *Sexual Anarchy*, Elaine Showalter writes that the New Woman "engendered intense hostility and fear as she seemed to challenge male supremacy in art, the professions, and the home" (38). There are female stereotypes of passion and frailty in Martí's poetry. There is also an enduring nostalgia for woman as guardian of the home, a partner in man's struggle for life. There is unease and anxiety before the rapidly changing role of women in the northern metropolis. There is, however, none of the harsh ridicule that was the general response to women's struggles for equality.

In Martí's defense of different styles of writing, the opposition between "feminine" and "masculine" is maintained but neither term is privileged over the other. In the essay in the Venezuelan magazine, written in 1881, Martí describes writers, intellectuals, poets, people like himself, as "workers of the mind"—*trabajadores de la mente*. It is still a male category, but one that is more inclusive and more open-ended than the common feminine/masculine contrast. Martí goes on to describe an attraction between these "workers of the mind" that recalls Whitman's erotic camaraderie, although Martí's essay on the poet, written in 1887, was several years away: "Who can contain this irresistible sympathy that drives us, as if toward a beloved brother, toward he who, weary from a burning inner demon, casts it from himself in resolute prose, or in winged rime? Are they not all searchers of the truth, with lamps of different colors?" (7:199).

Martí's inclusive image, based on sympathy among "workers of the mind," is undone by a correlative image of "letters," that is, the literary arts, as "generous mothers on whose knees the fleeting quarrels of her sons are pacified." Nonetheless, rather than a univocal machismo that repels the feminine as a feared contaminant, there is in Martí a recurring tension between conventional images of gender polarities and the possibility of questioning such polarities.

In other words, Martí's unease regarding the changing role of women cannot be merely read as the recalcitrant misogyny of a nineteenth-century "man of letters." Rather, such an unease must be read in the context of a larger, ongoing preoccupation in Martí with the relationship between the emotional and the political, or differently put, the relationship between the private affections of an individual's body and the social, political body, that is, the citizens of a republic. Martí never formulated a definitive statement on this topic; on the other hand, he returns to it throughout his works, in polished essays and in unpublished notes.

Martí's goal was not merely the liberation of Cuba but the liberation of all bodies that would make up a new republic. His unfinished project included the possibility of transforming human relations in a revolutionary social and political setting. Martí suggests that this was to be a liberation not just of ideas but of bodies; however, for him the body is also an impasse, and he retreats from it, into the more familiar and safer rhetoric of a sublime, spiritual human bond.

The poet Walt Whitman, perhaps the one Martí most admired, had cut through this impasse with a new language, distilled in the radical poems of the protean *Leaves of Grass*. Martí was "probably the first Latin American to respond to Whitman's seduction with the kind of enthusiasm that feared its own gasping for breath" (Sommer, "Martí, Author of Walt Whitman" 78). Not only in his famous essay on Whitman, but in other references and appropriations, Martí's admiration and debt are evident, along with a telling anxiety before Whitman's joyfully transgressive embrace. In an article subtitled "José Martí Reads Whitman," Sylvia

Molloy writes lucidly of "Martí's highly circumspect, ambiguous read-ing—gravitating toward dangerously attractive poems while distancing himself from them" (376).

Martí's essay, "The Poet Walt Whitman," was published in Mexico in 1887. However, Martí's earliest comments on Whitman were published in November and December, 1881, in the Caracas journal *La Opinión Nacional*, the same journal in which he wrote about the seasonal dances in New York City. Martí arrived in New York in January 1880. In March of the following year, he went to Venezuela, with plans to lecture and edit his *Revista Venezolana*, mentioned above. He returned to New York in July 1881, and by August, he began sending notes on various topics to *La Opinión Nacional*, first under a pseudonym, then using his own name. The articles for Venezuela's *La Opinión Nacional* offered Martí the opportunity to touch on hundreds of topics, some dealing with cur-rent events, others with cultural and literary novelties. The format pre-figures that of a popular magazine, stocked with a series of sharp commentaries on every topic imaginable.

Martí's early comments on Whitman suggest a recent discovery that he is eager to share with his readers. In his 1881 note for the Venezuelan journal, Martí writes that original drama is not having much success in the United States. On the other hand, Martí goes on, there are admirable poets, who write "with great power, grace, tenderness and originality. . . . A great variety of topics and great honesty in their tone characterize their poetry. They mix the profound and the delicate, the cheerful and the sad: and so their verses achieve color and the appear-ance of life" (23:81). In this praise of the new poetry of the United States, Martí inserts a brief but significant comment on Whitman, who was preparing the 1881 edition of *Leaves of Grass:* "A poet from the United States, famous for the daring of his rhymes, the boldness of his thought and the freedom of its form, a freedom at times approaching disorder, is watchfully preparing a collection of his works in the univer-sity city of Boston, in the cultured and pretentious Boston. The poet is W[hitman]" (23:81).

Beginning with this early comment, Martí mixes unconditional praise with a sense of unease before Whitman's radically different poetic uni-verse. From Martí's point of view, Whitman's "freedom" in form and content borders on *descompostura*, "disorder," but literally translates as "breakdown," "decomposition" and "untidiness." In all his subsequent comments on Whitman, including in his groundbreaking essay, despite his admiration Martí never abandons an unresolved ambiguity regard-ing Whitman's radical proposal for liberating bodies from the confines of stale categories. Yet Martí continues in his praise of Whitman, calling him "the greatest poet, rebellious and powerful" in a letter (December 1882) to Bartolomé Mitre, the venerable editor of *La Nación* and former president of Argentina (9:18). In fact, among his many book projects, Martí mentions one to be titled *Los poetas rebeldes* (the rebel poets), which was to include essays on Whitman and Oscar Wilde.

Martí again wrote about Whitman in December, 1881, also for *La Opinión Nacional*. Again he refers to Whitman as a "rebel poet," who takes things to the limit, and that limit is set by the demands and desires of the body: "Walt Whitman, the North American poet rebellious to all forms, who sings in a tender language, full of the shades of the moon, the things of the heavens and the wonders of nature, and celebrates with spring-like nakedness, and at times with paradisiacal daring, the rude, carnal forces that act on the earth" (23:128).

It is clear from this early comment that Martí recognized the transgressive power of Whitman's project. With uncommon insight, Martí also recognized that this power is grounded on human desires, not on derivative ideas or principles. Thus, no ready-made poetic form can contain such energy; new forms must be found to express it. Martí appropriates and translates, in the broadest sense, the liberating spirit of Whitman's lifelong project. On the other hand, Whitman embraces not just "mankind" but the body of a real man, in love and in death, while Martí seems to struggle with the body's desires, wherever they might take it. In Martí's republic, the common good is always superior to the "dangerous, exclusive contemplation of trivial personal tortures" (7:209). Martí never wavers in his praise of Whitman's poetics of liberation, but he struggles with an American individualism grounded on the body, on the irrationality of its needs, its desires and its ineluctable decay. Paradoxically, in Martí the body takes center stage on the eve of death, on the eve of its final dissolution in nature.

In "José Martí Reads Whitman," Molloy argues that Martí anxiously misreads Whitman's "intimations of homosexuality," making them all the more obvious, despite "a compulsively heterosexual justification whose violence cannot be ignored" (378). However, Molloy concludes that "Martí is the only Latin American to have considered in Whitman, the erotic together with the political and to register his anxiety, even his panic, before that explosive alliance" (379). In his essay on Whitman, Martí focuses on Whitman's most homoerotic poems, the "Callamus" cluster. Martí comments on the "material, brutal, corporeal form, with which [the poet] expresses his most delicate ideals." He immediately adds that such a language has seemed "lascivious" only to those incapable of understanding its greatness. Martí is explicit in his denial of "vile desires" in *el amor de los amigos* (love between [male] friends), implying that it is, or should be, a strictly Platonic affair.

As Molloy has pointed out, Martí's ambiguous reading of "Callamus" highlights, rather than erases, the homoerotic charge in Whitman's poems. Whitman places "adhesiveness" at the heart of democratic ideals that are grounded on the desires of individual, diversely gendered bodies, not on the abstract aspirations of a paradoxically incorporeal, genderless, idealized body. Martí appropriates Whitman's "adhesiveness" as a democratic principle, but in his writings, friendship between men is more valuable than carnal love between men and women precisely because such (male) affection is beyond the desires and the implicit disorder of the physical body. Martí's praise of (male) friendship is most succinctly expressed in one of his *Versos sencillos* (simple verses): "Si dicen que del joyero/ Tome la joya mejor,/ Tomo a un amigo sincero/ Y pongo a un lado el amor" (If they tell me, from the jeweler,/ To take the best jewel,/ I take a sincere friend/ And set love aside). Male friendship is Martí's marriage of true minds.

It is hardly a question of faulting Martí for his inability to embrace what Michael Moon has called "Whitman's privileging of male-homoeroticism in the political program of *Leaves of Grass*" (228). What is significant is that Martí stops on the threshold of his own version of a politics of the erotic, inspired by Whitman, but carried to its own natural conclusion. In Martí's project, the need for a marriage of true minds among virtuous men is clear and predictable. The role of women is another story, and Martí's comments about the women's congress underscore his admiration as well as his anxiety. However, if "woman" represents an impasse in Martí's approach to the politics of the erotic, he shows a willingness to consider new arguments. There is evidence of a positive evolution in his thinking about women and their new role in society, an evolution cut short when all of his energies went into the struggle for Cuba's independence.

Further evidence of Martí's increasingly progressive attitudes are found in an 1889 review of *Jonathan and his Continent: Rambles through American Society*, a book on the mores and customs of the United States by French writer Paul Blouët, using the pseudonym Max O'Rell. In a rather lengthy review of O'Rell's book, Martí focuses on the development of what he calls "another type of woman" in the North, that is, in the United States. O'Rell had written humorously about sophisticated women who marketed their "graces" to the highest bidder, "a disabled old man or a plain forty-year old" and thus secured their financial future. Martí does not disagree with O'Rell's portrait; yet he immediately launches into a description of a different "type" of woman in the North:

But there is also in the North another type of woman, strange and almost ineffable, about whom Tocqueville no doubt said that he saw in the superiority of woman the key to the North American nation. Because of her, although the terms are still confused and indefinite, perhaps there may be found a balance, in the intense sum of her disinterest and her feelings, for the evident lack in man, and in woman herself, of these national values.

Pero también es del Norte ese otro tipo de mujer, extraño y casi inefable, por quien dijo sin duda Tocqueville que veía en la superioridad de la mujer la clave de la nación americana, y por quien, aunque confuso e indefinido todavía, acaso se equilibre, con la suma intensa de su desinterés y sentimiento, la carencia patente en el hombre, y en la mujer misma, de estos valores nacionales. (12:156)

In other words, this "new type" of woman will balance out, or supplement, something that is lacking in both men and women. Some women may lust after "superfluous luxury." At home, she may not be "the decorous companion and intelligent friend that she could be"; on the other hand, in the United States, only a "new type of woman" possesses "the virtuous strength that may "compensate for the disorders of power, and the sordidness and roughness of life, which seem to be the destiny of American man" (12:156). Again, Martí seems to borrow the rhetoric of the women's movement, discussed by Cott and many others. In the arguments of early advocates for women's right, "both sexes would benefit if women were to gain *equal* access to education, work, and citizenship" (Cott 19, her emphasis). Although for Martí, "the terms [of equal access] are still confused and indefinite," it was a confusion and lack of definition that was not entirely absent from the early women's movement itself.

Significantly, in Martí's comments about the New Woman, "man," however briefly, ceases to be a universal category; rather, "man" is gendered in order to underline his difference from woman, whose qualities outstrip his. Not just any woman, and evidently not the trophy wives ridiculed by O'Rell, but socially and politically committed women are having an impact on the values and the direction of the republic. Martí writes:

In that apostolic life of celibacy, in the new dignity of reasonable marriages, in the courage with which she faces ridicule, in the physical and moral strength with which she presses forward her political, artistic and literary campaigns, in the surprising harmony and originality of her intellectual works, in her relative disinterest, always superior to that of man, one may see the only flowering of that Christianity, the only evidence of that pure leaven, which will soon be indispensable to hold back this new Rome, when it begins to degenerate, and to crave, like the Rome of the Caesars, all the flora and fauna of the world for its table and to fill its reservoirs.

En esa vida apostólica de celibato, en la dignidad nueva de sus casamientos de razón, en la bravura con que afronta el ridículo, en el vigor físico y moral con que lleva adelante sus campañas políticas, artísticas y literarias, en la armonía y originalidad sorprendentes de sus trabajos mentales, en su desinterés relativo, pero siempre superior al del hombre, se ve el único retoño de aquella cristiandad, el único asomo de aquella levadura de pureza, que será dentro de poco indispensable para sujetar a esta nueva Roma, cuando empiece a degenerar en sí, y a querer, como la de los Césares, que toda la flora y la fauna del mundo le llene los manteles y le nutra los estanques. (12:156)

The "degeneration" of the United States into a greedy new "Rome" may be checked by "disinterested" women, that is, those engaged in social and political struggles. Martí moves from gender differences and sexual politics to suggestions for reigning the power of the United States, an ever-expanding empire, whose next step, as Martí points out throughout his writings, might very well be Cuba. According to Martí, the expansionist policies of the United States, cast in the role of a "new Rome," must be checked and redirected, for such policies translate into a squandering of resources on all fronts, moral, financial, and political. The task of checking the unbridled expansion of the empire falls on the "new type" of woman praised by Martí: "androphobes, passionate poetesses . . . or angels with spectacles," who work not only for the benefit of other women but for men. Martí recognized the political potential of the women's movement to grapple not only with the inequities of gender politics but with a broad spectrum of issues, which together would determine the future of the United States, and would surely impact on Cuba's own struggles for independence in the shadow of its mighty, ambitious neighbor.

In many of Martí's comments on marriage, he suggests that ideally marriage should be a relationship based on understanding and cooperation, qualities that were ultimately absent from his own marriage. In an unpublished note, in a notebook dated 1880–1882, Martí wrote a poignant critique of conventional marriage, proposing a model that might have pleased the early advocates for the reform of marriage:

It is taken for granted that the basis of love is an element that cannot sustain a marriage: physical attraction. A quick external impression presides, almost exclusively, over the vehement expressions and serious promises that have become indispensable conditions of love. And, there is such a difference between liking and loving each other! One should follow the

example, putting aside all malice, of certain Indians from the state of
Veracruz [Mexico], that is, take each other on trial. To live under the same
roof. To go together to the creek. To carry kindling together. To listen to
each other and get to know each other. And if the definitive sympathy
between souls does not sanction the fleeting attraction between bodies—
then separate from one another. The balance between the conditions of
each member of a couple, and their mutual recognition, are the only conditions for good fortune in marriage. To do otherwise is to gamble your
life by flipping for heads or tails. (21:233)

In this fragment, Martí redefines marriage as a willing participation in
a human bond, valid as long as love and mutual cooperation persist.
Marriage based on physical attraction and subsequently sustained by
mere convention or convenience is an unprofitable, onerous burden.

Martí's most radical, most suggestive thoughts on gender differences
are found in his comments about the "primitive arts" of Native
Americans, in an essay published in New York's *La América* in April
1884. The conquistadors "robbed a page from the Universe" because
they violently cut the development of flowering civilizations: it was "a
historical misfortune and a natural crime" (8:335). For native people,
the Milky Way was " 'the path of souls,' and the Universe was full of the
Great Spirit, in whose bosom there was all light, the rainbow crowned
by a crest. . . ." Martí concludes by contrasting the Biblical tale of Adam
and Eve with a native version of the creation: "These were people who
did not imagine, like the Hebrews, woman made from a bone and man
made from clay; rather both [were imagined] as born at the same time
from the seed of the palm tree!" (8:335).

In this native fable of origins, woman's primal dependency on man is
replaced by an image of equality, which echoes in Martí's comment
about marriage as a partnership of equals. In other instances, woman as
frail, yet treacherous temptress, reappears, a version of the "false Eve" of
the poems, a hindrance to "man's" spiritual journey. In his vast, fragmentary, richly suggestive text, Martí did not resolve such paradoxes or
polish them for inclusion in his ideal republic. Yet he shows an uncommon willingness to listen to what the speakers at the women's congress
had to say.

Martí often set the stereotype of the Latin woman in an idealized, and
frankly nostalgic, vision of home and family. On the other hand, northern women were described in a variety of roles: opulently dressed beauties, lonely working women, survivors of shattered families, defenders of
woman's rights. The Latin stereotype of woman is not defined in social
or economic terms, but rather in conventional aesthetic terms (woman
as "elegant lily") and on vague images of home and family. By contrast,

the northern woman in Martí's essay is clearly the product of specific social, political circumstances.

Working women in the North are battling poverty, and in his essays Martí deliberately slips from working women to poor people in general, both coming into the world as the "sickly branches of an ailing tree, which sprouts between a rickety table and a glass of beer, and hears from birth bitter words, and sees somber things, and is frightened by them, and walks alone" (9:248). In this passage, Martí moves from working women to a genderless image, the sickly tree, which represents human struggle in adverse circumstances, the product of the painful inequities of the northern metropolis, which affected men, women and children.

By 1882, Martí's own situation in the city was closer to that of his emblematic tree, struggling to survive, than to the idealized image of home he associated with the now-distant values of Latin people. Carmen Zayas Bazán, Martí's wife, resented his ever precarious financial situation and his constant work. Martí's biographers have written of his struggle to reunite his family in New York. In a letter written to Bartolomé Mitre, editor of *La Nación*, in December 1882, Martí paints a fleeting but memorable image of his home life in New York: "But after two years of not seeing my wife and son, they have come to me during these very days, in the midst of this raw December, to brighten my little house, recently set up" (Pero después de dos años de no ver a mi mujer e hijo, me han venido en estos mismos días, en medio de este crudísimo diciembre, a alegrar mi casita recién hecha) (9:17). In 1885, Zayas Bazán went back to Cuba with her son, not returning until June of 1891 (Toledo Sande 214). By August of the same year, Zayas Bazán again decided to leave her husband, and, without his knowledge, sailed for Cuba with her son. The family would never be reunited.

In the absence of his wife and son, Martí found a partner, *una compañera*, in Carmen Miyares de Mantilla, the woman to whom he wrote one of his last letters, suggesting various projects that might help her and her children to survive and entrusting her with his papers. The relationship between Carmen Mantilla and Martí is the source of an unresolved debate regarding the paternity of María Mantilla, the daughter of Carmen and her husband Manuel Mantilla. In a recent biography, Toledo Sande concludes that Martí unofficially adopted the young María, his goddaughter, and that he became the companion and soulmate of the widowed Carmen, but only after her husband's death in 1885, when María was five years old. In his *La vida íntima y secreta de José Martí* (Martí's intimate and secret life), Martí scholar Carlos Ripoll agrees, arguing that Manuel Mantilla was not a feeble old man, as commonly held, but that he remained active until his death at the age of 42. The opposite arguments are the subject of a book by José Miguel Oviedo, who points out that in her later years María herself, claimed Martí as her biological father. In another twist to the question of María Mantilla's paternity, her son, the late actor César Romero claimed Martí as his grandfather.

In Julio Ramos's persuasive interpretation of Martí's "family crisis," the Puerto Rican critic suggests that in Martí's writings a "broken home" is compensated by other forms of filial relationships, evident in the bonds between father and son in *Ismaelillo*, and the bonds between (male) friends that are a strong pillar of a democratic republic. According to Ramos, Martí suggests new schemes, new social and political configurations, which "at times take on the familial form, precisely in order to *redeem* the failures of traditional structures before the impulse of modernity" (*Divergent Modernities* 198). Whatever its precise nature, in his relationship with Carmen Miyares, her daughter María and her other children, Martí also reconstructed his own broken family life, in part the result of shaky "traditional structures" that he subtly but insistently questions in some of his writings.

What role would women play in new social and political structures, rising from Martí's meditation on the crisis of the family, his own and those of society? One may conclude that whatever role a woman might have taken—virtuous virgin, fecund mother or faithful companion—the position of women in Martí's writings remains subservient to men. On the other hand, Martí's comments on changes in women's roles suggest a positive evolution in his thinking, from early, rather coy comments on New York's "manly women" to a thoughtful, if brief, presentation of the women's movement in the 1880s.

Writing for Latin readers, Martí was a pioneer in recognizing the value of the proto-feminist agenda, summarized by one of speakers at the women's congress. What is more remarkable is that Martí acknowledges the political potential of women's voices in a democratic republic. It was not merely the voice of a victim, but a voice advocating changes that might transform a nation, a voice defending the rights of all workers and capable of holding back "this new Rome." At the same time, Martí never retreats from his anxiety regarding the changes in women's roles that he witnessed in New York City. The city was far from the Cuban countryside, where a war of independence had to be waged. Martí dedicated his efforts to the struggle for a free Cuban republic, guaranteeing the rights of black and white men. The participation of women in such a struggle was obviously secondary to that of men, economic and moral support, on the one hand; on the other, there was the iconic image of the heroic woman, epitomized by the matriarch of the Maceos. In preparation for a war in Cuba, the question of race and racism took center stage.

CHAPTER 3

AGAINST RACE

As a young boy in Cuba, probably in 1862, when he was nine years old, Martí accompanied his father, a circuit captain in the service of the Spanish crown, on trips to the countryside and to the villages surrounding the city of Havana. Martí's father had been assigned the impossible task of preventing slave ships from docking in Cuba. Although slavery was not abolished in Cuba until 1886, Spain, often pressured by England, had agreed to put an end to the slave trade as an erratic, half-hearted prelude to abolition. During one of the trips with his father, the young Martí saw something that haunted him for the rest of his life, an image he immortalized in one of the poems in his *Versos sencillos* (simple verses). During a fierce storm, a slave ship unloaded its human cargo on Cuba's shore: "Echa el barco, ciento a ciento,/ los negros por el portón" (the boat's great door disgorges/ Negroes by the hundreds) (*Selected Writings* 281). The boy then saw men, women and children packed like chattel in windowless barracks. He saw a screaming mother running off with her baby: "Una madre con su cría,/ Pasaba, dando alaridos." He saw the body of a man hanging from a tree, a man who had tried to run away and paid with his life. "A child saw that," the poem concludes. At the feet of the dead man, the child swears "to wash that crime away with his own life" (Lavar con su vida el crimen). Martí's dream of justice and equality is grounded on this horrific vision of a lynching in the Cuban countryside, witnessed by a nine-year-old boy.

Fast-forward from the Cuban shores of Martí's childhood to New York City's Coney Island in the fall of 1881. The trains and ferries disgorged thousands of people on the shores of the newly built amusement park. City dwellers flocked to the beach in search of fresh air, ready to put down money for thrilling rides and newfangled soft drinks. Martí published his impressions of the amusement park in an article for Bogotá's *La Pluma* (the pen), December 3, 1881 (9:121). Surrounded by the voices and laughter of the crowd, Martí was saddened by a sorry sight. He saw how "an unfortunate man of color" was paid "a miserable wage" to put his head through a hole, so that customers could take turns throwing a ball at his nose. A hit was greeted with hoots and hollers, while the poor man grimaced grotesquely as he tried to dodge a direct hit.

The two images taken from Martí's experience, the slave ship in 1862 and the carnival worker almost twenty years later, define two distinct horrors: a violent death and a life of indignity. Those two images were branded in Martí's mind, and it was his intention to pass that mark on to his readers. In his writings Martí preserves his memories of a dead man hanging from a tree and of a man paid to degrade himself, yet he did not write to preserve memories but to change reality. While living in the United States, Martí witnessed the progressive unraveling of the promise of emancipation and equality for all. He fought for the creation of a republic where people would triumph because of their merits and their efforts, not because of the color of their skin or the texture of their hair. In other words, Martí dreamed of a future nation, one he did not live to see, but his faith in that possibility has not lost the power to move us.

Much has been written on Martí and the topic of race. The various readings of such a complex topic have evolved over the years, producing disparate and even contradictory readings. In an elegant understatement, scholar Paul Gilroy writes that the topic of race, enclosed in what he calls "scare quotes," presents "a delicate situation," adding that "'race' remains fissile material" (4). It would take a hefty monograph to review the topic of race in Martí, its historical context, its repercussions in Cuba and Latin America and the many readings it has generated. It is a collective work-in-progress, which covers from Fernando Ortiz's appropriation of Martí's anti-racist thinking (Helg) to contemporary objections about Martí's erasure of race for the sake of a narrative of national unity (Ferrer). In an article titled " 'Martí y las razas' (Martí and race): A Re-evaluation," Martínez-Echazábal synthesizes Martí's "poetics of 'race,'" as well as Ortiz's assessment of it in his book, *Martí y las razas.*

After a brief overview of Martí's writings on Native American cultures and on immigration, this chapter considers the impact that racial politics in the United States had on Martí during the years he spent in this country. It focuses on Martí's unique take on the topic of "race and reunion" in the years following the Civil War, a topic discussed by contemporary historian David Blight. Martí wrote forcefully and frequently about the evils of using so-called racial qualities to oppress people and set one group against another. In articles, speeches and proclamations, he insisted that racial prejudice would do irreparable damage, if not destroy, his dream of a democratic republic in Cuba. Yet Martí's preoccupation with race and race prejudice was not limited to Cuba, its history and its political future. While living in the United States, from 1880 to 1895, Martí saw firsthand how racism and race hatred were destroying the democratic ideals he admired.

In the title of Paul Gilroy's *Against Race: Imagining Political Culture beyond the Color Line*, published in 2000, there is a remarkable echo of Martí's own writings "against race." In a climate of prejudice and race hatred, Martí worked to suggest the power of a "strategic universalism," Gilroy's term. Today that vision is perhaps no closer to reality than it was in Martí's time; yet it remains pertinent, indeed it is urgent, to restate one's faith in its potential.

According to historian Eric Foner, by 1900, five years after Martí's death, "the ideals of color-blind citizenship and freedom as a universal entitlement had been repudiated" in the United States (131). Between 1880 and 1895, while living in New York and travelling frequently on the eastern seaboard, Martí witnessed an alarming contraction of civil liberties that in the case of African Americans had turned into a reign of terror. As the failures of Reconstruction crystallized into a segregated society, race hatred exploded across the land, from the violent outbursts of white supremacists to the sometimes genteel yet entrenched racism of all public institutions. In the North, segregation in all spheres of society was taken for granted, while distinguished scholars published pseudo-scientific studies on the superiority of one race over another. During the 1880s and 1890s lynchings took place in unprecedented numbers, while in some cities African Americans began to organize themselves to demand justice and access to public institutions systematically closed to them.

In her pioneering work on the persecution and killing of African Americans, Ida B. Wells-Barnett (1862–1931) pointed out that in the late 1880s and early 1890s, lynching became a prominent feature of race relations, especially in the states of the old Confederacy. In 1892 Wells-Barnett herself was forced to leave Memphis because of her protests against racism and segregation. The offices of her newspaper, *Memphis Free Speech and Headlight*, were burned by a mob. That same year, while living in Philadelphia, Wells-Barnett published her first pamphlet, "Southern Horrors." Subsequent studies on racial violence in the nineteenth century, for example, by Raper in 1933, Ayers in 1984, Williamson in 1986 and Dray in 2002, agree that in the late 1880s and early 1890s lynching took center stage as a frequent, violent expression of race hatred.

Martí knew that racism was more than an Achilles' heel in the struggle for Cuban independence: It was a gaping wound. If the wound would not heal in time for an attack on Spain, at least it had to be exposed and cleansed, in the hopes of a future healing. The metaphor of a wounded body is apt, and Martí knew that the healing would be a painful process, but one that any nation thus afflicted had to face. It has often been said that Martí was an idealist, yet his analysis of racial prejudice in his own time was convincingly argued and solidly grounded on his own experience. Moreover, his wish for racial harmony was no pipe dream but a real desire and an absolute requirement for any nation where democracy might be worthy of its name. What may seem idealistic or even naïve to us today is that in the face of prejudice and hatred, Martí offered an unwavering sense of hope for the future.

Martí often wrote about Native Americans in the United States and in Latin America, about the marvels of their culture and the persecutions they endured, volatile topics as Martí discovered in Guatemala. In 1878 Martí published a book on Guatemala, in which he wrote admiringly of the art and traditions of native people, revealing, he said, "unknown riches." The book turned out to be fodder for Martí's enemies, who found his democratic ideas threatening. His teaching duties at the university were reduced, and Martí's friends and collaborators were dismissed from their posts. In April, 1878, he left Guatemala in disgust, writing to his Mexican friend Manuel Mercado: "Con un poco de luz en la frente no se puede vivir donde mandan tiranos" (with a little light on your forehead [in your mind] one cannot live where tyrants rule) (20:47).

The people native to the North American continent, Martí wrote, are right to refuse to pay the costs of a citizenship that they do not enjoy. They are weary of laws written in a language that they do not understand (10:374). Martí defended the Native Americans' right to land and liberty and wrote admiringly of the legacy of the civilizations native to our continents. "The [European] conquerors," he writes in an article on American antiquities, "stole a page from the Universe." In other words, they trampled the wisdom of a people for whom the Universe "was full of the Great Spirit" (8:335).

In 1882, Martí deplored a congressional proposal to exclude Chinese immigrants from San Francisco and other western cities: "It was the mortal duel of a city [San Francisco] against a race. In order to uphold the enslavement of Negroes, the South waged war. Well then, in order to achieve the expulsion of Chinese people, the West would have gone to war" (Por mantener la esclavitud de los negros hizo una guerra el Sur. Pues por lograr la expulsión de los chinos hubiera hecho una guerra el

Oeste) (9:282). With great admiration Martí quotes the arguments of those in the Congress of the United States who opposed the closing of doors to a "respectful, useful and peaceful race." There were those who argued in vain that "to forbid the entrance of any man, or an entire group of men, to this land, was like tearing with a dagger the generous Constitution of these people" (9:282).

In Latin America, the native populations that had survived centuries of persecution and genocide lived on the fringes of a culture in which race prejudice was the norm. In Cuba, the slave trade continued until the middle of the 1860s, and slavery lingered until 1886. In the United States, racism was tolerated when not blatantly encouraged. During his lifetime, Martí's cry for equality and justice was echoed by the reformers he admired. He eulogized abolitionist preachers Henry Ward Beecher and Wendell Phillips. In 1882 Martí wrote a compact review of the autobiography of Frederick Douglass (1818–1895) calling it an "anatomy of the spirit" (23:212). Douglass's autobiographical narrative, first published in 1845, was expanded in an 1881 edition, the one reviewed by Martí. It should be added that a few years later, Martí condemned the aging Douglass for his support of a United Sates plan to take over Haiti and the Dominican Republic.

At the same time, Martí was not "exempt from stereotyping" (Helg 45). Especially when he wrote about the various immigrant groups in the city, Martí depicted Chinese, German and Jewish people in broad, journalistic strokes, sacrificing the individual for the sake of a type easily grasped by readers at that time but crude and even offensive today. Moreover, it has been convincingly argued that Martí identified the "disorders" of the city with its immigrant populations, "layers that cannot cohere" and that presented a threat to his ideal of national unity (Kaye 73). In an article glossing a book about immigration, Martí writes that the best immigrants are those who are educated and skilled; those who are not and who come "loaded with appetites," are given to drinking and crime. He concludes that "an immigration that cannot be assimilated into the country should not be encouraged" (8:384). Martí presents stereotypical images of some of these "uncultured" immigrants, but his main concern is that immigration is a serious social problem that is not receiving sufficient attention.

To a great extent, the conflicts between ideals of national unity and the specific interests of various groups still define the politics and culture of the United States. It is no wonder that such conflicts troubled Martí and that he considers them central to an understanding of the United States in the years following the Civil War. The situation Martí faced in dealing with racism in Cuba and in exile groups in the United States took all of his energies and of course called for entirely different strategies. These strategies involved persuasion and tactical compromise rather than direct confrontations, for reasons that I hope become more obvious as this chapter unfolds.

Another cogent objection to Martí's ideas regarding race has been raised by Cuban historian Rafael Rojas, who refers to what he calls Martí's "paternalistic creole mentality" in some of his notes and book projects regarding "the black race" (114). According to Rojas, Martí remains faithful to "a republican principle," which asserts that distinct "races" should not form separate entities but must come together in a "national civic community." Moreover, such a civic community "demands the disappearance of racial identities" (Rojas 115). This is an important point, but it does not mean that Martí believed that race, as it was known at the time or as we know it today, would disappear in an ideal citizen, transformed by education and civic virtue into a homogenous entity. It does mean that "color" or any other individual characteristic, whether racialized or not, must have no value in any definition of citizenship worthy of the name. This is the core message of Martí's essay "Mi raza" (my race), discussed below, where Martí argues: "We seek and find an essential similitude, beyond differences in the details. What is fundamental in analogous characters fuses in various parties, even if [such characters] differ in incidental ways, or in ways that may be deferred for the common good" (Lo semejante esencial se busca y halla, por sobre las diferencias de detalle; y lo fundamental de los caracteres análogos se funde en los partidos, aunque en lo incidental, o en lo postergable al bien común, difieran) (2:299).

In Martí's street scenes of New York City, the snapshot of a national type sharpens the panorama of the immigrant masses. There is the angry Irishmen, the restless Swede, the wily Jew—stereotypical images taken from the jostling crowds of the great metropolis. Yet, as Schulman points out in an article on "ethnic and cultural minorities" in Martí, there is also praise for the contributions of the many groups that made up the teeming city (149). What touched Martí the most, however, for it had marked him since childhood, was the treatment of people of African descent in the United States and in Cuba. In letters, essays and even in his poetry, he wrote passionately about the need to stamp out race prejudice. Martí saw racism as a kind of inner exile, a corrosive evil that destroyed both the hater and the hated.

Martí countered prejudice with an almost evangelical credo grounded on the ideals of justice and equality. He stated his beliefs in many articles and speeches, most notably perhaps in the *Manifesto of Montecristi*, written on the eve of his final departure for Cuba as one of the leaders of an expedition destined to rekindle war against Spain, discussed in the final chapter of this book. In this document, written in Montecristi, in the Dominican Republic, Martí describes the "foolish fear, disguised as prudence and fueled by cowardice," that some white people have for black folk. "In the Caribbean heart," he writes, "there is no hate," no hate between blacks and white, not even hate against the Spaniard. Hatred is reserved for tyranny and injustice (4:96–7). As historian Ada Ferrer has shown, during the wars for Cuba's independence, 1869–1898, there were instances of cooperation and mutual respect between blacks and whites, and there were also instances of prejudice, hatred and mistrust. Martí was well aware of the painful legacies of insurgent Cuba. He called for unity for the sake of independence, not only because it was politically expedient to do so but also because he felt that it was morally reprehensible to do otherwise.

For Martí no argument spoke louder against the enslavement of human beings than the corpse hanging from a tree that he saw as a child. No book could explain what he saw; no tradition could account for such a horror. Only the act of witnessing sufficed, and Martí wrote simply that a child saw that dead man: "Un niño lo vio." Martí knew that Cubans of African descent must play an active role in the republic he hoped to found. He also knew that many white Cubans feared the participation of black Cubans in the struggle for independence, for it might lead to their dreaded presence in the affairs of the new republic. Even as their control of Cuba slipped away, Spanish authorities fed the long-standing fears of white landowners that the participation of men and women of color in the struggle for independence would have dire consequences. Fears of a "black republic" in Cuba's eastern provinces, and of a replay of Haiti's revolution, in fact thwarted the spread of the independence movement during the Ten Years' War (1868–1878), (Pérez 120–6; Ferrer, especially Part I). In the United States, "racism permeated the Cuban exile and immigrant community," according to Nancy Mirabal in an article focusing on Martí's "politics of unity" in Tampa, Florida.

Although estimates vary, the participation of black Cubans was central to the struggle for independence from its beginnings. According to one estimate, 70 percent of soldiers in the Ten Years' War were black, while Cubans of African descent made up about 32 percent of the entire population (P. Foner, *Antonio Maceo* 312). Moreover, many individuals of African descent were promoted to the rank of officer. Yet the top leadership of the independence movement "belonged to the white race," Foner's phrase.

On the subject of racial prejudice, and the possibility of harmony among people of all races, Martí wrote a compact, much anthologized essay titled "Mi raza" (my race) first published in New York's *Patria*, on April 16, 1893. From Key West to New York City, from Philadelphia to Tampa, Martí tirelessly raised funds as he organized an armed expedition to Cuba. He knew that only a unified front could hope to put an end to Spain's grip on Cuba and Puerto Rico. The fractious bickering within the ranks had to end; otherwise, Spain, fighting fiercely to maintain its hold on the Caribbean, could not be defeated.

In "Mi raza," Martí writes that *racista* is a confusing word, which must be clarified. No one has the right to say "my race" if by saying so he or she means to proclaim the superiority of one human being over another. What is "a sin against humanity" is whatever divides us from each other, whatever sets us apart or corners us (2:298). In a series of rhetorical questions aimed at various factions within pro-independence groups, Martí argues that a sensible person should not feel vain because of his or her color. To insist on differences between people in order to separate them is to violate the republic, to do violence to the public trust. Martí believed that to violate the rights of one individual was to violate the rights of all. In brief, that was his definition of freedom. Freedom for one person at the expense of another was no freedom at all. In other words, Martí believed in Lincoln's ideal of national unity. If Reconstruction had trampled on that ideal, it was a calamity for all the people of the United States, for decades to come. Cuba, Martí hoped, might follow a different path, and if not, he would do everything in his power to at least leave a map that future generations might have the wisdom to follow.

Martí often wrote on the ways that the legacy of the war between North and South played itself out in his own time. In an insightful reading of Martí's essay on Ulysses Grant, Díaz-Quiñones writes that "The North American Civil War, with its political and literary prestige, opened a space that was especially attractive to Martí's epic imagination during the 1880s." In his writings on Grant and the Civil War, Martí delves into the relationship between war and democracy, between militarism and the ideals of a modern republic, between the hero and the writer. These are the central issues in his own development as a political thinker. As Díaz-Quiñones and others have shown, Martí took advantage of issues that were central to the history, the culture and politics of the United States to formulate his own vision for Cuba and Latin America. On the question of race and its attendant prejudices and hatreds, the United States during the 1880s offered ample opportunities for reflections on a topic that was central to Martí's development of multiple strategies to carry out the "necessary war" that would bring independence to Cuba.

In the years following the Civil War, instead of the promised freedom, African Americans faced hatred and exclusion at every turn. Martí wrote that every day black people were murdered in the South and excluded in the North, "avoided and persecuted in the country of their birth" (esquivados y perseguidos en el país donde nacieron) (11:237). In 1882, two years after Martí's arrival in New York City, the *Chicago Daily Tribune* began keeping records on lynchings, a pioneering project essential to all subsequent research. An article published in New York's *Sun*, on July 7, 1887, under the headline "The Race Prejudice," gives specific details on the topic as it played itself out in northern urban centers. The article describes a "mass meeting of the colored people in one of their churches uptown to protest against the treatment of their race at Asbury Park." According to the article in the *Sun*, in northern cities, "White people refuse to go where they will be brought in contact with large numbers of Negroes, whether it is a church, a theatre, or a watering place. That is the fact, and enfranchisement and the Civil Rights bill have in no respect altered it." In the United States, Martí saw the damage done to democratic ideals by the contraction of citizenship along racial lines. At the same time, he also witnessed the beginnings of the Civil Rights movement in the efforts of African Americans to turn anger and resentment into organization and protest.

In an article published on August 16, 1887, Martí contrasts the legacy of Lincoln with the racism of his own time. The article is Martí's prescient version of some of the issues treated in David Blight's *Race and Reunion: The Civil War in American Memory*, published in 2001. In his article, first published in the Buenos Aires daily *La Nación*, Martí writes about a Fourth of July reunion between "the Blue and the Gray" in Gettysburg and about a bloody battle between blacks and whites in Oak Ridge, a hamlet on the outskirts of New Orleans.

New York newspapers published reports of both events, which Martí used as sources for his own article. Yet there is an important difference between the accounts of these events in the New York press and Martí's own version. For the New York dailies, a celebration of national unity in Gettysburg and a skirmish in a race war in New Orleans had nothing to do with each other. For Martí, the two events represented two sides of the same coin: the sad reality of race relations in the United States. Journalism in the United States figured prominently in Martí's "invention of the *crónica* (chronicle)," a hybrid genre, precariously but efficiently situated between reportage and essay (Rotker). Discussing Martí's version of another incident of ethnic violence in New Orleans, directed at a group of Italians, Julio Ramos aptly refers to Martí's technique as a "deconstructive use of citation" of the New York press

(*Divergent Modernities* 111, n58). Martí's linking of Gettysburg and Oak Ridge may then be called a deconstructive juxtaposition.

As Blight points out in *Race and Reunion*, by the 1880s the myth of national reconciliation was often represented in the sentimental reunion between the North and the South, and in the many statues and plaques erected to commemorate such events. It was, Blight writes, a white reconciliation that deliberately erased the realities of slavery and the participation of African Americans in the war that officially ended it. In his article Martí recognizes the pathos of the 1887 reunion at Gettysburg, the victors offering their hands to the vanquished. However, Martí does not stop at the undeniable aesthetic impact of such a scene. In fact, in an unprecedented move, Martí links the scene of reunion at Gettysburg with the horrors of race prejudice, the very facts that the white establishment was eagerly erasing from national consciousness, despite the efforts of African American veterans and the embattled defenders of the legacy of emancipation.

On the front page of the edition that published articles about the Fourth of July 1887 celebration in Gettysburg, both the *New York Times* and the *Sun* carried prominent stories about a bloody incident in Oak Ridge, Louisiana. Neither paper considered the relationship between the two incidents, one a grand celebration of national unity and the other, a "racial" incident in a remote corner of the nation. However, Martí eagerly seized on the contrast between the ideal of national unity, represented with great pageantry in Gettysburg and an example of the "Southern horrors" described just a few years later by Wells-Barnett.

The celebration at Gettysburg was attended by hundreds of Civil War veterans from both sides of the Mason-Dixon Line, their families and the widows and children of the dead. A special guest was the widow of General George Pickett and her son. On Sunday, July 5, the *New York Times* published a front page article entitled "Mrs. Pickett's Reception," calling the widow of the famous Southern general, "the center of attraction in the field." The article on Mrs. Pickett included the following headline: "Union and Confederate Veterans Comparing Notes on the Scene of their Memorable Struggle." On the same page with the article on the Gettysburg reunion, the *Times* published an article entitled "The Oak Ridge Riot: Twelve Negroes and One White Man Killed." Martí wrote his article for *La Nación* on July 8, just three days after the stories appeared in the New York press. In a telling juxtaposition, he combines "race and reunion": race hatred versus the sentimental reconciliation of the two great armies.

In his article Martí describes the "magnificent parade" during the Fourth of July celebration in the famous battlefield at Gettysburg, an occasion for pageantry and grandeur. It was a solemn commemoration of the nation's unity on land that had been the site of the battle, on July 1–3, 1863, that changed the course of the Civil War, a place hallowed by the memory of Lincoln's most famous words: "Four score and seven years ago. . . ."

Martí presents an image of somber reconciliation, a contrast to the horrors of war still fresh in the minds of the survivors. Martí asks his readers to imagine what those survivors of the Great War might have been thinking: "What about my missing arm?"; "What about the missing bone in my chin?"; "What about my brother?" Reconciliation could not erase the painful memory of war, yet they all marched in respectful silence, Martí writes. Sometimes the adversaries shared the same carriage, and in silence, they shook hands. The band played the songs of both armies (11:236).

In his article on the Fourth of July at Gettysburg, Martí paints a memorable portrait of the event. Like a good journalist, he focuses on individuals to highlight the pathos of the situation. Veterans from both armies, the North's and the South's, visited the battlefield together, the place where "death reached as high as the sky." "Who does not remember the hopes of General Lee," Martí writes, "the frenzied charge of the men in gray; and their encounter with federal troops high on the hill, face to face. Who does not remember the grand and melancholy disaster of the southern army? Who does not remember their general [Robert E. Lee], walking alone, with something on his face approaching the divine cast given by death, moving between the trenches full of bodies? Who does not remember him walking among the wounded, who held their cries on seeing him pass, while the full moon shone with its merciful light?" (11:236).

In this passage, Martí echoes the sentimentality and pathos of Lost Cause writers, who, as Blight points out, were crafting a righteous version of Southern defeat, one where the aesthetic polish of selective memories masked the political realities that were in fact leading to legal segregation. In 1896, a year after Martí's death, the infamous *Plessy vs. Ferguson* Supreme Court decision declared that segregation did not violate the Constitution of the United States. Martí dwells on the glorification of a defeated South and the pageantry of the occasion, but he is laying the groundwork for a charge of his own against the racism at the heart of the land of Lincoln.

Various speakers at the celebration in Gettysburg took paints to present a "New South," heroic yet forgiving. Martí wants his Latin readers to see the theatricality and hear the rhetorical grandeur of the reunion. Yet, in a rhetorical flourish of his own, he suddenly switches to another topic, which apologists for the South were taking great pains to avoid: the enduring legacy of racism. It is a topic that had been absolutely banished from this stately reunion, and many others like it, but for Martí the two events were inexorably linked.

Martí writes that the same day of the parade in Gettysburg, other men, armed to the teeth as if ready for war, also marched in Oak Ridge. Their rifles are held high; their bullets are ready to strike the enemy. They look like bandits, but they are the sheriff and his gang, who have come to kill the Negroes of Oak Ridge, to punish them because a black man from the town "lives in love," *vive en amor*, with a white woman. Details of the incident appeared in two front-page articles published by the *New York Times* and the *Sun*, both on July 5, 1887. Significantly, the *Sun* and the *Times* give different reasons for the circumstances that led to the bloody confrontations in Oak Ridge. The reporter for the *Sun* writes: "A negro was accused of holding improper relations with a young white woman," suggesting that, however "improper," the relationship was consensual. On the other hand, the *Times* article says that "a colored man [was] charged with assault on a white woman." "Improper relations" become an "assault," the sort of sleight-of-hand that often led to the torture and murder of hundreds of African American men. Martí rejects both versions and makes a significant change in presenting the alleged relationship between a black man and a white woman. In both articles and in Martí's version, however, the outcome is the same. As a posse of white men led the accused man toward the jail, a group of black men fired on them. A white man was killed, and others were wounded. A series of armed confrontations followed. In the end, the death toll included the white man and twelve black men, who were killed in the fighting or else lynched after being captured.

In the newspaper articles and in Martí's version, the contradictory terms used to refer to the relationship between a black man and a white woman are revealing. In *Vengeance and Justice: Crime and Punishment in the Nineteenth-Century American South*, Edward Ayers discusses radical changes in relations between the races. According to Ayers, in the early years of Reconstruction, whites feared that freed blacks would organize to demand justice, resorting to violence if necessary. He mentions a group of blacks organized into a "regular army company" to avenge the murder of a black man in 1867. By the late 1880s, however, the fears of Southern whites began to focus on what Ayers calls a "a new crime," namely, the alleged assault and rape of white women by black men. Thus the alleged rape of white women by black men became a regional "phobia," Ayers's term. Supposed assaults on white women, or rather the perception that such assaults were commonplace, became the prime justification for the epidemic of lynchings that began in the final years of the nineteenth century.

In Wells-Barnett's pamphlets and in subsequent studies, the stereotype of the defenseless white woman, whose honor had to be protected by men, is linked to the lynch-mob mentality of the period. In his version of the incident for Latin readers, Martí transforms the white woman and the black man into a couple who "live in love." For that love, not only was the black man murdered, but all the blacks of Oak Ridge had to be punished. "The sheriff and his patrol have come to kill the Negroes of Oak Ridge as punishment for the fact that a Negro from that place lives in love with a white woman," Martí writes (11:237). No doubt Martí realized that whatever may have happened in Oak Ridge, in a climate of prejudice and hatred, a relationship between a black man and a white woman, whatever its character, could become the justification for mob violence. In these circumstances, lynching did not violate the law; it became the law. Only in the pioneering work of African American critics and in subsequent historical research can one find anything comparable to Martí's lucid reading of racism and its violent consequences in the United States.

Martí writes that in the South, "not a day goes by without bloodshed." In the North, the Republican Party pretended to defend the Negro, so that with their vote they would be assured of victory in elections against the Southern states. Losing political ground because of the Republican strategy, the South seethed at the North. Martí writes that Lee, the governor of Virginia, had a solution: "he would throw all the Negroes into a burning pyre" (que de los negros todos haría una llamarada) (12:336). Martí is referring to Fitzhugh Lee, Virginia's governor from 1886 to 1890, a nephew of Robert E. Lee and himself a general in the Confederate Army. Significantly, Governor Lee also served as a general during the Spanish-American War, in which his tactics for dealing with black people were eventually put into use by white rulers fearful of another U.S. intervention. More on this later.

Two years after the Gettysburg reunion, Martí wrote an article in which he expresses his hope for a harmonious future in the United States. In September 1889, at a public celebration in Boston marking the anniversary of the Emancipation Proclamation, a young black man read the famous document out loud "with a voice that rang in the air like the echo of a hammer on steel" (La leyó un negro joven, con voz que vibraba en el aire como el eco de un martillazo sobre acero) (12:336). In these essays, "race and reunion" in Gettysburg and Oak Ridge, and the celebration in Boston, Martí synthesizes the past, the present and the future of "the question of race" in the United States. In the past, there were the horrors of slavery and the Great War that it unleashed. In the present, Martí's present, there was reunion at Gettysburg, while elsewhere the most brutal forms of racism thrived and expanded. For the future, there was the hope of a young man in Boston with a ringing, powerful voice, reading the Emancipation Proclamation.

Martí asks us, his readers today, to share his awe at the reconciliation on the Fourth of July at Gettysburg by directing our gaze to the human drama unfolding in the battlefield. He brings our attention to the image of the widow of Confederate General Pickett, who spearheaded the attack by leading 5400 hundred soldiers, "*los grises*" (the men in grey), in a doomed charge against the Union's relentless cannons. Walking on the field where thousands lost their lives, the widow of the man who led the charge up to Cemetery Hill gathered some daisies and clover leaves and, like an aging Ophelia, handed them out in memory of the day to Federal and Confederate soldiers alike.

From an image of sorrow and sympathy for the defeated, the widow and her son, embracing and crying (*lloraban abrazados*), Martí takes us back to the incident in Oak Ridge and then to a brief yet charged summary of the situation of people of color in the United States. The dramatic force of the contrast points at once to the greatness of Lincoln's nation and to its tragic flaw: "It is the dawn of a formidable problem" (Es el albor de un problema formidable) (11:238). Surely reconciliation at Gettysburg was a noble thing, and eloquent words were spoken on the occasion. "Today, soldiers of the contending armies, we meet as citizens of a united country," said one of the speakers at the ceremony, as reported in an article the *Sun* (July 3, 1887), entitled "Reunion at Gettysburg. Survivors of the Blue and the Gray Unite in a Camp Fire" (10). However, it goes without saying that this desired national unity was hardly inclusive, and that those whose exclusion was most glaring were African Americans, consigned to a genteel invisibility, when they weren't being lynched in Oak Ridge and hundreds of places like it.

At the ceremony in Gettysburg, one Captain Reeve from Richmond, a commander under Pickett, spoke of the need to "bury in oblivion the bitterness and hate of past strife." Colonel William Aylett, from Virginia, continued in the lofty tone required by the occasion: "Above the ashes left by the war and over the tomb of secession and African slavery we have created a new empire" ("Reunion at Gettysburgh"). What sounded like poetic grandeur to the white audience gathered on the famous battlefield must have come across as so much hot air to the young black laborers who worked setting up the stage and other accouterments. In these segregated events, "the only role for blacks was as laborers" (Blight 386).

Poetic grandeur or not, the underlying message of the veterans' long-winded speeches is explicit in the words of Colonel Alexander McClure of Philadelphia: "It was a strange, sad conflict. Men of the same race, inheritors of the same heroic traditions, sovereigns in framing the same laws, met in deadly struggle to solve great civil problems." In other words, white men had fought a necessary war not over slavery but over "irreconcilable theories," and a greater Union, ruled by white men, had emerged from the mighty struggle, "its jarring pillars cemented by the arbitrament of the sword" ("Reunion at Gettysburgh").

By contrast, Martí believed that the situation of African Americans was central to the stability and prosperity of the nation. Their parents suffered the disgrace of slavery, Martí writes, but by now their children displayed the character and intelligence of a free people. In his article about the ceremony at Gettysburg, Martí even touches on a topic that has been recently discussed: the question of reparation for the sufferings of slavery. Martí writes unequivocally that "they are owed, of course they are owed, reparation for the offense [of slavery]" (Se les debe, por supuesto que se les debe, reparación por la ofensa [de la esclavitud]) (11:237). Martí writes that poverty, not race, makes people ignorant, and so black people must prosper and grow in strength in order to survive. In a passage that might have been written by W. E. B. Du Bois, whose classic *The Souls of Black Folk* was first published in 1903, Martí writes:

> They [African Americans] buy land and houses; they found banks; they uphold their own beliefs and create their own universities; they fortify themselves in their own communities; they defend themselves, like those unfortunate people in Oak Ridge, with a gun on their arm.
>
> Compran haciendas y casas; fundan bancos; levantan credo propio y universidad propia; se fortifican en sus pueblos: se defienden, como los infelices de Oak Ridge, con el arma al brazo. (11:238)

Countering Martí's cherished ideals of national unity, this statement calls for an enlightened form of separation as a way to deal with hatred and exclusion. If African Americans are persecuted and despised "in the country of their birth," that is, is in their own nation, they have a right to struggle against it, by founding institutions and even by taking up arms.

And what happened in Oak Ridge? Fire and gunpowder, deaths on both sides. Four black men lay dead in the field. Eight were lynched. And who will punish the sheriff, Martí asks, since he is the law? Answering his own question, he concludes: "He must be cleaning his rifle for another hunt" (Para otra cacería estará limpiando el rifle) (11:238).

In "Mi raza" (my race), Martí writes of a "just racism," which means "the rights of blacks to maintain and prove that color does not deprive them of any of the capacities or rights of the human species" (2:298). At the same time, Martí feared that an emphasis on racial differences would not lead to equality but to fragmentation. He also writes of "white racists" and "black racists," who provoke each other by isolating themselves. They are both "enemies of peace."

In the cautious language of today, one would be justified in saying that Martí's discussion of race and racism is controversial. It may be argued that while recognizing and admiring cultural plurality, Martí proposed if not an idealized erasure of racial difference then at least its deferral for the sake of unity in the struggle for Cuban independence. Yet one should reconsider the context of Martí's writings on race. "Mi raza" is not a theoretical treatise on a controversial topic. It was a call to arms, written, as Martí would say, on the arm of a chair, before he darted to yet another fundraiser or to a raucous political meeting, where his enemies were ready to discredit his next move.

Two years, almost to the day, after the publication of "Mi raza" in New York's *Patria*, on April 16, 1893, Martí's dream of an armed invasion into Cuban territory was realized. Along with five others, including Dominican General Máximo Gómez, he landed in Cuba on April 11, 1895. On May 19, on a charge against the enemy, Martí was shot and killed. "Mi raza" is part of a long prelude to that death. It is a call to fight a common enemy, not merely Spain but oppression and injustice under whatever flag they might cower. Martí's words on race and race prejudice are a cry from the heart, amplified by the knowledge that racism would destroy the Cuban republic, making a mockery of all the ideals of justice and equality that Martí and two generations of Cubans had fought and died for.

In "Mi raza" Martí asserts: "In Cuba, there is no fear whatsoever of a race war" (2:298). Martí knew that such a fear existed, yet his assertion is not false. On the contrary, it represents a desire rather than a fact. The force of such an assertion put the question of race on the table and might thus influence the course of events. It is remarkable that against all odds, and in the face of the brutal, increasingly institutionalized racism of the very country that he admired as a model of democracy, Martí imagined a Cuban republic free of racial hatreds. In one of his most famous, and controversial, declarations, Martí argued that to be a Cuban "is more than to be white, more than to be mulatto, more than black" (2:299). Taken out of context, the statement may be read as a willful erasure of difference for the sake of a national ideal free of thorny contradictions. On the other hand, in the context of Martí's lifelong struggle against hatred and prejudice, the statement is both a political challenge and a visionary ideal. Martí's greatest fear was that history would indeed repeat itself. During Cuba's first war of independence, the interests of white landowners prevailed over unconditional emancipation, a fact that figured prominently in the failure of the independence movement and the reaffirmation of Cuba's colonial status. During the war of independence that Martí was organizing, lingering prejudices and hatreds based on "racial" differences might have similar consequences.

Martí's worst fears came true 17 years after his death. In the first decade of the twentieth century, black Cubans, many of them veterans of the war for independence, organized in order to oppose their increasing exclusion from the political process of the republic they had helped to found. According to Tomás Fernández Robaina, author of *El negro en Cuba 1902–1958*, the *Independientes*, members of "The Independent Party of Color," felt that in "Martí's doctrine of equality" lay part of the solution to the problems of prejudice and racial discrimination in the new republic (104). The crackdown against the *Independientes*, prompted in part by the fear of U.S. intervention, was swift and ruthless. In about a month—June 1912—some three thousand black Cubans were murdered. One of the officers in charge of the operation described it as "butchery": *una carnicería*. In *Our Rightful Share: The Afro-Cuban Struggle for Equality 1886–1912*, Aline Helg examines the participation of black Cubans in the struggle for independence and studies the events that led to the atrocities of 1912. A photograph of the massacre included in *Historia de Cuba* (564) shows a row of bodies hanging from the same tree: Martí's childhood vision of a single corpse hanging from a tree had been horribly multiplied. There was indeed no race war in Cuba. There was instead a massacre of black Cubans who had dared to organize to improve their situation.

Martí's plea for the unconditional inclusion of people of color in a democratic republic was grounded on a fact known to all: Cubans of African descent had participated in the struggle for independence since its beginning. It was evident that it would be immoral to include some of those who had fought for freedom and exclude others because of their race or their class. What was less obvious to many, though it was clear to Martí, was that the exclusion of those who had fought for independence would be politically disastrous. In "Mi raza," Martí advances his arguments against racism by grounding them on the heroic participation of freed slaves in the first war of independence (1868–1878), led by white landowner Carlos Manuel de Céspedes. In Martí's narrative, heroism and freedom are joined in the martyred body of the emancipated slave. It goes without saying that the facts of the participation of black Cubans in the independence movement were more complex, but Martí was not writing history. "Mi raza" is a political treatise and a call-to-arms. It is the work of a poet turned political activist. It was indeed, as Lugo-Ortiz has written, a recasting of the Ten Years' War as a narrative of national unity (136).

Martí's writings "against race" offer a counter-image to the social fragmentation, racism and class warfare of the United States. His essays and comments on this topic were an attempt to create a tactical narrative on the eve of a war, not only a war against Spain's old-school colonialism but against a new world order increasingly controlled by the most arrogant, most belligerent forces in the United States.

According to historian Louis Pérez, the terms of emancipation during the Ten Years' War were far from clear. Eastern landowners recognized that freed slaves were needed in the war against Spain; however, in Cuba's western provinces, landowners were generally unwilling to support a war that might risk their economic stability. They were even less willing to link such a war to the abolition of slavery, which would have a disastrous effect on the plantation economy. Eventually, even after a murky compromise on the question of slavery, the war remained largely confined to the eastern provinces. "Not all slaves emancipated by insurgent operations," Pérez writes, "obtained either freedom or equality" (*Cuba* 123). However, historical details were blurred in order to produce an enduring national legend centered on the image of Céspedes, the landowner who freed his slaves so that they might fight for independence.

The story of Céspedes and his freed slaves became a national myth, short on details, long on ambiguities, yet powerful in its dramatic impact. It became a staple of the history lessons taught to generations of Cuban school children, this writer included. In this familiar version, at the dawn of our long struggle for independence from Spain, on October 10, 1868, Céspedes, the white landowner, freed his slaves so that they might join him in a war against a common enemy. Evoking the image of Céspedes, Martí writes in 1893: "In our battlefields, they died for Cuba, and the souls of white people, the souls of black people, rose together through the air" (2:299). The image is simple; its message, clear. Equality in death must mean equality in life. At the same time that Martí evokes Céspedes's famous gesture, he also echoes the voices of other independence leaders, notably Máximo Gómez, who felt that "the invasion of the west [of Cuba] was linked directly to the abolition of slavery, and both were vital for Cuban success" (Pérez, *Cuba* 124).

In "Mi raza" Martí focuses on an image of equality and national unity, not on the specifics of Céspedes's famous gesture. As the leader of

Cuba's fight against Spain, Céspedes needed the financial backing of white landowners. At the same time, he needed to free the slaves so that they could join the fight. In order to have it both ways, Céspedes proclaimed a decree of abolition limited to those slaves willing to join the fight against Spain. Céspedes's plan did not succeed in obtaining financial backing from most landowners, but the link between independence from Spain and the end of slavery, between freedom for Cuba and freedom for all its people, had been made.

During the Ten Years' War, landowners remained fearful that a war with Spain would damage their lucrative business interests, and they needed slaves to work, not to fight a risky war. What is more, they feared that slaves armed to fight against Spain would one day turn their weapons on their former masters and transform Cuba into a "black republic." Spain seized eagerly on this fear and made it central to its propaganda against the insurrectionists. Many of the landowners were in fact lobbying for alternatives that would be less radical than absolute independence from Spain. To avoid a costly war, Spain might be persuaded into easing its political grip on Cuba in exchange for economic stability and a hefty slice of the pie. Another plan, dreaded by Martí and many Cuban patriots, yet long cherished by the landowning class, revived the possibility of asking the United States to incorporate Cuba in its prosperous federation of states.

In a chapter of Cuban history that was certainly omitted from the public school curriculum, Céspedes himself considered annexation to the United States as a way to obtain independence from Spain and avoid the devastation of a lengthy war. As historian Ada Ferrer has shown, fears about the possibility of "a bitter war of the races" played an important role in the desire to consider an independence mediated by the United States.

Moreover, Céspedes and other rebel leaders were far from unambiguous regarding abolition and slave participation in the war against Spain. According to Ferrer, Céspedes deferred abolition, while privately confiding that "Cuban slaves were not yet trained for freedom" (29). The war itself, Céspedes argued, would be a training ground, where former slaves would learn "the proper meaning of true liberty" (Ferrer 29). Nevertheless, in Cuban mythology, the image of the slave, freed to fight against a foreign tyrant, was enduring. In this idealized narrative of Céspedes's famous gesture, the slave gained his freedom by fighting for it alongside white Cubans, both united against the same oppressor. Martí had to pay homage to Céspedes's heroism and at the same time assure his supporters that fears of a "race war" were unfounded. Such fears, he argued, were the anachronistic legacy of the Ten Years' War, grotesquely inflated by Spanish propaganda.

A central point in Martí's arguments "against race" is grounded on the legendary equality of the battlefield, where blacks and whites died together. As historians have shown, there was hardly equality in Cuba's wars of independence. On the other hand, Martí stresses that there is equality in the willingness to face death for a worthy cause. From this point he can then argue that people are to be judged according to their character and not their color. That certainly seems obvious to us, but in 1893 Martí was writing against a racism so entrenched, so "normal," that the inferiority of people of color had become a given, a fact so "natural" as to be beyond all discussion. The fact that such racism was explicitly linked to the political and territorial expansion of the United States was certainly not lost on Martí. According to Reginald Horsman, author of *Race and Manifest Destiny*, "[b]y 1850 American expansion was viewed in the United States less as a victory for the principles of free democratic republicanism than as evidence of the innate superiority of the American Anglo-Saxon branch of the Caucasian race" (1).

Wherever people gather to form a group or a political party, there are divisions, Martí writes, but "affinity of character is more powerful than affinity of color." Black or white, those driven by pomp and self-interest will go to one side; those driven by generosity and disinterest will go to the other. "Together they work," Martí concludes, "whites and blacks, for the cultivation of the mind, for the dissemination of virtue, for the triumph of creative work and sublime charity" (Juntos trabajan, blancos y negros, por el cultivo de la mente, por la propagación de la virtud, por el triunfo del trabajo creador y de la caridad sublime) (2:300).

After Martí's death, his progressive agenda was watered down in the policies of a republic designed to advance the interests of the economic elite and their most powerful allies: U.S. business enterprises eager to expand their control of the Cuban economy. Today progressive people agree that diversity is a healthy thing in any society, and tolerance for difference is part of the guarantee of basic rights for all people. Martí would of course agree, but he also called for a common ground of human decency and cooperation as the cornerstone of any free republic. He needed to forge a strong coalition to oppose a common enemy, but he was not merely thinking of what would be tactically advantageous. He insisted on an essential core of human dignity common to all, regardless of differences "in the details." Such differences were admirable when they proclaimed the richness of humanity; they were damnable when they led to exclusion and isolation.

From Mexico to Key West, from Tampa to Philadelphia to New York, Martí relied on the collaboration of thousands of men and women who contributed generously to the cause of Cuban independence. However,

there were two men Martí could not do without: Máximo Gómez and
Antonio Maceo. Gómez (1836–1905) was a retired general, a brilliant
strategist and a veteran of the Ten Years' War. In 1878, when efforts to
continue the war of independence failed, Gómez returned to his native
Dominican Republic, where he lived on a tidy farm with his family.
General Maceo (1845–1896) had been a prosperous Cuban landowner;
then, as a legendary leader in the Ten Years' War, he refused to concede
defeat in 1878, thus setting the stage for the eventual rekindling of the
independence movement. Martí had to convince a war-weary Gómez to
return to the battlefield. He had to nurture an alliance with Maceo, and
at the same time placate the fears of white Cubans, especially the exiled
leadership, that a black man in such a powerful position, commander of
the insurrectionist army, would ultimately undermine their own interests.

In 1878 the Ten Years' War ended with what Maceo called a "dis-
honorable surrender." The Pact of Zanjón, as the surrender came to be
called, had been worked out between Spanish authorities and a "com-
mittee" of Cuban leaders that did not fully represent the opinions of the
insurrectionist leadership. According to Ferrer, "among the principal
Cuban architects of the peace [with Spain] was [Cuban insurgent]
Marcos García . . . who had lamented the rebellion's appeal to Cubans
of color" (63). In what would become a heroic chapter in Cuban history, Antonio Maceo refused the terms of the surrender and continued
fighting. Spanish authorities did not hesitate to bring "the race question" into their attacks on Maceo, "an arrogant mulatto" who insisted
on the absolute abolition of slavery as a condition for laying down arms.
Maceo was finally forced to leave Cuba, but he refused to call his departure an official surrender. Thus the "pact" that ended the war with Spain
became a mere cease-fire, and Maceo and other exiled patriots continued working for Cuba's independence (P. Foner, *Antonio Maceo* 87).

On July 20, 1882, just four years after the end of the Ten Years' War,
Martí wrote Maceo from New York, asking him about his eventual participation in a renewed struggle for Cuban independence. In the letter,
Martí pays homage to Maceo for his fame as Spain's most feared enemy.
By that time, Maceo had settled in Honduras, where he was appointed
to important military and civil posts (*Antonio Maceo* 109). "I do not
know of a soldier braver than you," Martí wrote Maceo, "nor a Cuban
more tenacious than you. It would be incomprehensible to me that
anything serious might be done for the cause of Cuba, if you were
not included in the special and prominent way that is guaranteed by
your well deserved reputation." In this same letter, written from New
York, Martí frankly addresses the question of race prejudice (1:172).
According to Maceo biographer Philip S. Foner, among Cuban exiles

there were those, "influenced by a white-supremacist ideology," who sought "to limit the role of blacks in the revolution, and especially to prevent Maceo from assuming a commanding role" (*Antonio Maceo* 94).

"The solution to the Cuban problem is not political but social," Martí wrote Maceo, "and such a solution cannot be achieved without the mutual love and forgiveness of both races" ([esta solución] no puede lograrse sino con aquel amor y perdón mutuos de una y otra raza) (1:172). Such a solution cannot be achieved, Martí tells Maceo, "without the wisdom, always worthy and always generous, that I know lies in your proud and noble heart." Martí considered it "criminal," he told Maceo, "to smother the legitimate aspirations to life of a noble and prudent race, which has already suffered so much misfortune." Because the letter was addressed to Maceo, not to an audience or a group of readers, Martí's impassioned plea is especially moving. "You cannot imagine," he tells Maceo, "the very special tenderness I feel as I think about these misfortunes, and about the ways, neither vociferous nor ostensible, but rather quiet, active, loving, evangelical, to remedy them" (No puede imaginar Ud., la especialísima ternura con que pienso en estos males, y en la manera, no vociferadora, ni ostensible—sino callada, activa, amorosa, evangélica de remediarlos) (1:172). Martí knew that Maceo's body bore the many scars of battle and that his actions in the first war of independence had earned him fame and respect. He also knew that Maceo had been repaid with unkind words and racial slurs from the very people whose freedom and whose interests he had defended.

Much has been written on the differences between Maceo and Martí, the warrior and the poet, the man of action and the man of words. However, such radical polarities, though iconic in the national imagination, obscure the complexities of the relationship between these two men. Martí's relationship with Gómez was no less difficult. These three men shared the leadership of a revolution against Spain. It goes without saying that were tense disagreements among them, at times compounded by distance and precarious lines of communication.

Frictions between Maceo and Martí flared for the last time in 1895, as independence leaders gathered in Cuba's eastern mountains to coordinate their attack on Spanish rule. Martí wrote in his diary that Maceo's manner "hurts me and disgusts me." Maceo, the military hero, had misgivings about the influence of Martí, the poet and intellectual, with no experience in the battlefield. Pages from Martí's diary were torn out and lost forever, adding to the mystery. On May 19, 1895, two weeks after this final meeting with Maceo, Martí was killed in Dos Ríos, in the province of Oriente.

Along with Gómez and the revolutionary forces, Maceo, now fighting in Cuba's western provinces, went on to push the Spaniards to the brink of defeat. In January 1896, Maceo's troops were moving from Pinar del Río, Cuba's western province, to the province of Havana, immediately to the east. The *Times* of London noted, with glee no doubt, that Spanish control of Cuba was at an end. Maceo bitterly lamented the lack of equipment and supplies for his troops, yet he pressed on in one successful campaign after another. By the end of that year, in December 1896, General Maceo and his troops planned to attack Marianao, then a village on the outskirts of the capital, a prelude to final victory and a triumphant entrance into Havana. The attack never happened. Along with General Gómez's son, Maceo was killed during a minor ambush by Spanish troops. He was the last of five brothers who gave their lives for their country. Less than two years later, in the summer of 1898, Theodore Roosevelt and his Rough Riders were on San Juan Hill, at the eastern end of the island, in the province of Oriente. Almost overnight, Cuba's War of Independence became the Spanish-American War, a war between Spain, the fading empire, and the United States, a young nation with imperial designs of its own.

In 1902, after more than thirty years of war against Spain, capped by a U.S. occupation, Cuba finally emerged as a shaky republic, inexorably bound to the interests of the United States. After years of social upheavals and political uncertainties, the re-election bid of Cuba's first president Tomás Estrada Palma provoked an armed uprising in August 1906, followed by a three-year U.S. occupation of the island (Pérez, *Cuba* 223). A pamphlet entitled "Interesting Cuba," undated but probably published in the summer of 1905, captures the spirit of attitudes in the United States regarding Cuba. The writer of the pamphlet, Frederick A. Ober, praises Cuba's president Tomás Estrada Palma as "a bright example of what a Cuban ought to be, but isn't, for he has frequently proclaimed his island's indebtedness to the U.S. Still, through long residence in our country [the United States], Don Tomás is less Cuban than he is American. He is the Cuban—plus something better."

According to the author of "Interesting Cuba," the question of Cuban national identity revolved, paradoxically, around a surplus and a lack. Some Cubans lacked what Don Tomás had in abundance, that "something better" that made a mere Cuban into a national subject worthy of the trust and admiration of the United States. Today we are mistrustful of rigid notions of identity, confirmed by the artifice of boundaries or enforced by oppressive ideologies. We have learned to recognize the deliberate exclusions and the violence that have gone into the making of various identities. At the dawn of the Cuban republic, there is a significant turn on the question of national identity. It is not about what a Cuban "is" but what he or she "ought to be," and the arbiter in this trial of identity is the United States.

After the Spanish-American War, those in charge of the U.S. occupation of Cuba insisted that the interests of both nations would be served in a coalition between North American interests and the "better element" of the island. After a republic was established, Cuba's first president clearly belonged to that "better element." Many years of exile in the United States had made him that "Cuban—plus something better." He was "less Cuban than American," which also meant that he was fair-skinned, another positive quality to add to his patrician bearing and polished manner, not to mention his perfect English. In other words, Estrada Palma was a worthy representative of an elite whose fortunes depended in large part on its talents for collaborating with the government of the United States and mirroring the qualities it deemed essential for citizenship.

Just as Martí had feared, as the United States took control of Cuba, Puerto Rico and the Philippines, the racism directed at African Americans at home was exported and applied to the people of the newly conquered territories. Cartoons of the period, collected by John Johnson in *Latin America in Caricature*, portray Cuba, Puerto Rico and the Philippines as dark children, with the bulging eyes and huge lips of vaudeville's minstrels in blackface. In 1907, the *Detroit Journal* published one such cartoon, titled "Cuba's Freedom is Not Far Off." It shows a lanky Uncle Sam sitting on a stool on the shores of occupied Cuba, a sugar mill on one side and a U.S. battleship in the distance. Behind his back, Uncle Sam hides a limp rag doll labeled "Freedom," as he tickles the chin of a dark little girl with a huge, monstrously simian head. On the little girl's apron, she is identified as "Cuba" (Johnson 131).

In an 1897 book entitled *The Island of Cuba: A descriptive and historical account of the "Great Antilla,"* the authors offer explicit comments on the racial politics of American intervention: "Stigmatizing them [Cubans] as 'negroes' is, in part, at least, an appeal to the prejudices not yet extinct in this country" (Rowan and Ramsey 167). Outside the qualifiers, "in part, at least," there remains the "problem of race" in Cuba. The authors go on to reassure the reader that a captain from the United States who went to Cuba says they are "40% white, 40% Negro, and 20% of mixed blood" (167). The statistics are meant as an antidote to the caricature's portrayal of Cuba as a "Negro nation." After all, what U.S. interests really want out of Cuba is "[t]o have a peaceful, well-behaved neighbor, and a fair, honest customer" (218).

African American leaders were especially troubled by the racist agenda of the so-called Spanish-American war. According to historian David Blight, Lewis H. Douglass, Civil War veteran and son of Frederick Douglass, "feared that because Filipinos were so readily dubbed 'niggers,' American imperialism only meant 'the extension of race hate and cruelty, barbarous lynchings and gross injustice' around the globe among people of color" (Blight 349–50). When former slave and prominent Boston lawyer Archibald H. Grimké implored President McKinley to do something about the spread of violence against black Americans, he made an explicit parallel with the situation in Cuba. "Do the colored people of the United States," Grimké writes, "deserve equal consideration with the Cuban people?" (Blight 350–51). President McKinley ignored Grimké's petition.

In Cuba, Martí and Maceo became national icons, monolithic representations of an illusory national sovereignty. Martí was sculpted in white marble. Maceo was cast in bronze, the metal that was said to match the color of his skin. Every Cuban knows Antonio Maceo as "The Bronze Titan" of the struggle for independence, while Martí became known as "Cuba's Apostle of Freedom." Today such symbols of national identity, grandly sculpted and placed at the center of many a town square, are quaint reminders of another era. Yet we might reconsider the way that Martí's wisdom regarding the uses and misuses of "race" survived even as his dream of an independent, sovereign nation vanished.

As national politics became locked in a sterile polarity between conservatives and liberals, between left and right, Martí's wisdom endured underneath stilted eulogies to his martyrdom. Today the legacy of that wisdom may be the starting point for a reconsideration of what is truly progressive and just and what may offer a hopeful vision of equality and harmony. In a speech to a Cuban club in Tampa on November 26, 1891, Martí presented one of the most memorable renderings of this vision. Martí's speech was yet another call to arms, an impassioned plea for all to join in the struggle to free Cuba. As for "my Negro brother," Martí said, "others may fear him: I love him": (Otros le teman: yo lo amo) (4:277).

It was that fear, not the historical reality of race, which Martí sought to undermine. For Martí, racism led to an uncivil, unnatural isolation. "The white who isolates himself, isolates the negro," he writes in "Mi raza"; "[t]he Negro who isolates himself, provokes the white into isolating himself" (El blanco que se aísla, aísla al negro. El negro que se aísla, provoca a aislarse al blanco) (2:299). At a time when pseudoscientists studied the proportions of human skulls to create racist categories, Martí deplored the proto-fascist notion that proclaimed the "purity" of one race or another. He spoke forcefully against violence and oppression, justified in part by a belief in a "racial" pantheon ruled by the whitewashed deity of a fraudulent antiquity. In the United States Martí bore witness to the horrors visited daily on people of color. At the same time, Martí knew that many white Cuban leaders, just as they had in the aftermath of the Ten Years' War, would certainly hinder, or at best delay, the participation of black Cubans in a new republic. Martí protested with a powerful anti-racist credo whose echo still resonates with compassion and hope.

No one would argue that after Martí's death racism triumphed in Cuba. Martí's words, when they were remembered at all, acquired the rigor mortis of a dead canon, fodder for ideologues of every stripe, all proclaiming a vague, self-serving patriotism. For some, Martí's famous statement, "There are no races," became an excuse to ignore racism or to consign it to the realm of the invisible and the unspoken. Others saw it as a weakness in Martí's thinking, an erasure of racial differences and the hatreds it provoked for the sake of a shaky ideal of national unity. Such an interpretation of Martí is not only unjust but inaccurate, surely based on a partial reading of his works or on no reading at all.

The statement "There are no races" at the end of Martí's "Our America" is not an isolated, shortsighted affirmation. It is a vital part of a complex ideological strategy that also includes an unconditional belief in "the spiritual identity of all races," a level of human solidarity that certainly for Martí was not the sterile dream of a belated romantic but the real hope of a political visionary. Whether we can share that hope today is another story, or perhaps a series of stories in which hope and despair mingle in unpredictable ways. And yet we might still learn from Martí that hope for the future is not a vapid abstraction but a concrete option and a way to influence the outcome of real events.

CHAPTER 4

PAN-AMERICANISM'S EMPTY TRAIN

It was almost noon when the crowd got the first glimpse of the *City of Paris*. Folks had been milling around Battery Park since early morning, but the wait had been worth it, even in the September drizzle. It was indeed, as the newspapers proclaimed, a "palace of the sea," a "floating city," with seven hundred and eleven first-class passengers. Among those passengers were some of the delegates to the Pan-American Congress, set to open in Washington in just a few days, October 4, 1889.

There were those who praised the congress as the beginning of a new age of cooperation across borders. Others saw it as a bold move to secure subsidies for steamships and railroads. Whatever the opinions, however, the congress marked a turning point in the politics of the Western Hemisphere. When the congress opened, Martí was one of scores of delegates and attachés in attendance. When it closed, he had become the most important spokesman for Latin American interests of his generation. Long after his death, his voice continues to be heard throughout the Americas and his advice heeded on many fronts. Martí's understanding of the dangers and possibilities of hemispheric politics still rings true, long after the names of powerful organizers and prestigious delegates have faded into oblivion.

Like the special train that waited to take the delegates on a grand tour of the United States, the *City of Paris* carried its share of symbolic baggage. No doubt about it, the Inman Line steamer was the epitome of modern transportation. It was front-page news when the ship beat its own earlier record by a few hours. On August 29, 1889, the *New York Times* wrote breathlessly of the steamship's "record-breaking" trip, "five days, nineteen hours and eighteen minutes" from Queenstown, on the southern coast of Ireland, to Sandy Hook, at the mouth of Hudson Bay. "That the captain was anxious to lower [the earlier] record goes without saying," the *Times* reported. In order to save newly precious time, the ship followed the northern route, and the captain made sure it "should not deviate in the slightest from the shortest course." For those lucky enough to see it, as it lumbered into New York's spectacular harbor, the luxury steamer was an awesome image of the future. It represented two supreme values of modernity: speed and comfort. Excitement over new records set by steamers on their Atlantic crossings continued for over twenty years, until April 15, 1912 to be exact, the night the *Titanic* sank on its way to New York, closing a chapter marked by unprecedented confidence on the marvels of modern travel.

New York's business elite received the *City of Paris* and its Latin American delegates with great fanfare. In one of the articles he wrote for *La Nación*, Martí describes the occasion with the enthusiasm of a young reporter, but he had a far more important role to play during the coming months. As a delegate to the congress of American nations in Washington, he had to look beyond the fanfare. "The inner workings of this congress," he wrote, "are where such things always are: where you cannot see them" (Las entrañas del congreso están como todas las entrañas, donde no se las ve) (6:35). Martí was there to see, and to unite the Latin nations in a confrontation with their mighty host, to craft strategies for victory and to suggest ways to survive the asymmetries of power.

Soon after their arrival in New York City, the Latin American delegates were invited to make a grand tour of the United States in a special train, outfitted for the occasion. From Washington, they would travel to West Point, to see military things; on to Boston, to meet "men of letters" and see monuments; to Portland, Maine, to visit maritime industries. They would travel through the factories of New Haven and Hartford, Connecticut, and on to Springfield, Massachusetts; they would visit Albany, the state capital of New York. In Niagara Falls, they might "tune the spirit to great things," Martí wrote. Buffalo, Cleveland, Detroit, Chicago, Minneapolis, Omaha, St. Louis, Louisville, New Orleans and Pittsburgh were on the itinerary, a total of "five thousand four hundred and six miles."

The *New York Times* called it "the handsomest train ever put on rails." The first car was called "Esperanza" (hope); the others, including five Pullman cars, bore the names of various countries and historical figures. The train, the paper said, was as grand as the one used "for the Presidential party to come on to the recent Washington Centennial celebration." The *Times*'s description of the train's salons and vestibules is a precious summary of the period's taste for over-stuffed, plush interiors. It also gives a vivid image of the uses of opulence as a political tool: "The splendor of the interior decorations was well nigh palatial. Choice inlaid woods, blended in perfect harmony, formed the sides and tops. The furniture of mahogany and rosewood was upholstered with exquisite plushes and Orientally designed fabrics. In every nook and cranny was a piece of bric-à-brac or a pot of flowers . . . As a host Uncle Sam has proved himself to be an entertainer whose prodigality is only equaled by the good taste everywhere displayed" (*New York Times*, October 4, 1889:8).

Martí had been living in the United States for almost ten years before the Pan-American Congress of 1889. He did not need a ride in a fancy train to learn of the dazzling accomplishments of North American business and industry. He chose instead to learn about the workings of the congress and to try to understand the intentions of those who organized it, chief among them, James G. Blaine (1830–1893), Secretary of State under President Harrison. During a long career in politics, Blaine served as congressman from Maine from 1863 to 1876, ran for president on the Republican ticket in 1884, and twice served as Secretary of State. By the time he crossed paths with Martí, Blaine had been a central figure in national and international scandals. He had lost the presidency to Grover Cleveland in 1884 and was back on top as Benjamin Harrison's Secretary of State, his second turn in the post he had held under President James Garfield.

A year before the congress in Washington, Martí wrote an article on Blaine's performance at a political rally in New York. It was published in *La Nación*, on December 10, 1888. The rally was held at a baseball park, and the police had to use their sticks to keep the crowd behind the barricades. Powerful electric lights cast a hazy glow over a tide of human heads: "Garlands of flags, like colorful diadems set off by the gray sky, crown the top of the bleachers" (Coronan lo alto de la gradería, como diadema de color que se destaca sobre el cielo gris, guirnaldas de banderas) (13:359). In a rich collage, Martí gives his impressions of the rally:

> Outside, there are horns, fifes, drums, orange vendors, peanut stands, carriages coming and going, messengers in uniforms and blue caps, filling the hands of every passer-by with speeches, newspapers, denunciations, programs, caricatures, statistics, paper flags, historical summaries, quotations, portraits, circulars.
>
> You can walk for entire blocks over trampled papers.
>
> Afuera cuernos, pífanos, tamboriles, naranjeros, puestos de cacahuetes, carruajes que vienen y van, mensajeros de uniforme y gorra azul que le llenan las manos al transeúnte de discuros, diarios, denuncias, programas, caricaturas, estadísticas, banderas de papel, epítomes de historia, citaciones, retratos, circulares.
>
> Se anda cuadras enteras por sobre papeles pisoteados. (13:359–360)

Words are everywhere—shouted, whispered, printed, trampled under foot, but meaning is scarce. This was Blaine's territory. Martí writes how Blaine's well-timed entrance dazzled the crowd, who pushed and shoved to get a close look at "the man." In the heat of the moment, a journalist from a paper controlled by the Democrats screamed, "To hell with my newspaper! I'm a Republican!" (13:361). Martí is fascinated by Blaine's performance, but he does not hesitate to call him a "shameless sophist, a juggler of numbers" who can seem solemn, playful or sarcastic, as the occasion demands, like a great actor. Blaine "knows the art of speaking to a crowd." At a time when long-winded speeches were the norm, Blaine spoke for twenty minutes, left them cheering and was gone.

A great orator himself, Martí must have appreciated Blaine's gifts for winning a crowd, but behind the twisting of facts, the easy jokes and the theatrical gestures, he sensed arrogance and contempt. A year later, when Blaine spoke at the opening ceremonies of the Pan-American Congress, he used the same techniques Martí had seen back in New York. At the congress, Blaine's speech was designed to win over his opponents and appease whatever ill feeling may have been aroused by his election as president of the congress. Martí saw through Blaine's florid welcome and his praises of "the beauties of the excursion" in the fancy train. Martí knew that behind the scenes, Blaine had schemed to get elected to the presidency of the congress. The press, in the hands of his allies, referred to "Blaine's congress." As Martí saw it, Blaine was the prototype of the crafty politico, affable and persuasive, a beguiling speaker capable of winning an audience with the force of his personality, regardless of what message he had to deliver. Martí's portrait of Blaine is a portrait of the man as well as a compact manual on the power of political performance.

In one of his essay on the Congress in Washington, published in *La Nación*, on November 14, 1889, Martí describes Blaine as "a pale man, with piercing eyes and a lock of hair on his forehead, an imperious smile and soft hands" (Un hombre pálido, de ojo incisivo y cabello a la frente, de sonrisa imperial y mano suave) (6:42). His speech is dazzling, mellifluous and evasive all at once. He repeats the same phrase twice, with a different emphasis, in order to impress his listeners: the future will mean "more rapid communications" among our great nations. "What is marvelous about his speech," Martí writes, "is not its greatness, for there is none, but its prudence and the subtle way it answers objections before they are made" (Lo que del discurso maravilla no es la grandeza, que no la hay, sino la prudencia y el modo sutil de responder a las objeciones previstas) (6:43). Blaine's strategy is not to meet objections head on, but to say the opposite of what is expected, to say for example that "no one must be deceived in this congress" or that "there must be no secrecy among us." It's classic "newspeak," sixty years before Orwell coined the term. In fact, secrecy and deception lurked behind every potted palm. Opening his arms wide, his eyes riveted to a spot at the back of the auditorium, Blaine intoned, "seventeen republics have come together in peace and sincerity." He was a master of the well-placed, forcefully enunciated cliché. "Firm, suggestive, open, with a certain air of contained fury," Blaine knew the art of appearing "like a king, like a great soul, before weak people," just as he had done at the ballpark in New York the year before. Blaine's goal was to avoid whatever others might fear about him, and above all to leave a lasting impression of his "personal charm." "With a magnanimous gesture of his right hand," Blaine offered the entire country to the delegates, ending with a "welcome from Americans to Americans." The *Tribune*, Martí writes, "said that the applause was spontaneous, long and loud. Blaine owns the *Tribune*" (6:43).

It would be an understatement to say that Martí did not take Blaine's expansive gesture, welcoming the Latin American delegates to the United States, at face value. The real intentions of the United States were no secret to anyone, certainly not to Martí. Some newspapers referred to Blaine as the heir to "Clay's dream." An early advocate of Pan-Americanism as an antidote to the threat of European expansion, Henry Clay (1777–1852) opposed Jacksonian isolationists in an effort to develop "a system of which we shall be the center, and in which all South America will act with us" (Whitaker 32). As the heir to what editorials of the period were calling "Clay's dream," Blaine cast himself in the prestigious role of elder statesmen, eager to turn the United States into a world power.

Each Latin American nation brought its own agenda to Washington, and its delegates were unlikely to fall in line behind Martí. Yet he set himself the daunting task of persuading them to unite in the face of Blaine's plan to control the political and economic future of the Latin nations. The luxury train that awaited the delegates was designed as a symbol of North American comfort, hospitality and power, an awesome engine pulling behind carriages as plush as a courtesan's boudoir. As it turned out, the symbolism of the train evolved in unexpected ways. Some Latin American delegates came to resent it as they learned more about the plans behind the congress. Some U.S. newspapers, reflecting public opinion, saw the train as extravagant and wasteful, designed to coddle "our Southern neighbors," with taxpayers footing the bill.

However one might interpret its symbolism, the train was an impressive display of technology and luxury, the very emblem of progress. It had a bathroom, a barbershop, a library and a bar in one car; a French chef and five attendants in another. Martí remarks on the many servants on the train and admires "the feather bed, and the electric light at the head of the bed." The locomotive is a "wondrous thing, as safe as it is fast." There has never been a train as "comfortable or as ostentatious," he writes. Yet, "neither Argentina, nor Mexico, nor Chile . . . nor Bolivia is riding in it. The journey was too long for the delegates. They have stayed in Washington" (En él no van ni la Argentina, ni México, ni Chile . . . ni Bolivia. Era largo el viaje para los delegados. Se han quedado en Washington) (6:45).

It soon became clear to the Latin American delegates that the train had become a national joke, a "caricature" Martí called it. Local newspapers pointed out that it had been designed not only to impress the foreign guests but also to win over local politicians, eager to tout the prestige of their own cities. According to one account, quoted by Martí, the guests and their families took full advantage of the journey, "at the expense of the United States" (6:107). On board, the cigars were the finest, and the champagne flowed. In a preview of things to come, Washington's ambitious foreign policies were on a collision course with domestic interests. The train had a wheel in the ditch before it left the station, yet it plowed on. Martí's assessment of the increasingly militant foreign policy of the United States is blunt. Better for the Latin American republics to be "natural friends" of the United States than to become its "choir, subject to a country with different interests, a hybrid composition and terrible problems, determined to face the world in an arrogant, and perhaps childish challenge, before putting its own house in order" (coro sujeto a un pueblo de intereses distintos, composición híbrida y problemas pavorosos, resuelto a entrar, antes de tener arreglada su casa, en desafío arrogante, y acaso pueril, con el mundo) (6:53). Martí goes on to say that the United States has begun to consider that freedom, "a universal aspiration," is its exclusive privilege, "and to invoke its name in order to deprive other nations of it."

Even as a public relations disaster on wheels, the train symbolized progress as defined by the United States. Its message was clear: Either get on board or get run over. The *Sun* compared the train to a "Juggernaut," the mighty, mythical cart designed to crush all those who crossed its path. Martí quotes the New York daily's explicit commentary: "Whoever does not want to be crushed by the Juggernaut, let him come on board." Martí hoped for a different outcome: Rather than yield to it, better to "conquer might with intelligence" and to stand in the cart's way: "Mejor será cerrarle al carro el camino" (6:54).

In his writings about the Pan-American Congress, Martí never uses the first person. There is more than false modesty in this self-effacing stance. Martí had long been critical of the indifference of the United States toward Cuba's struggle for independence. He had become increasingly critical of the emerging policies of the United States toward Latin America. At the same time, Martí was organizing opposition to Spain's hold on Cuba from his exile in New York. It would have been politically unwise and even dangerous to bring attention to himself as the spokesman for Latin American interests in Washington. Nevertheless, there is no question about the importance of Martí's expanding role as a Latin American leader during the Pan-American Congress.

After all, the congress had some positive results. The American people, and some of its leaders, came to admire what Martí calls "the decorum of Latin people," (el decoro de los pueblos latinos) (6:108). There is no better way to push back those who prick our back, Martí told his Latin American colleagues, than to turn on your heels and face them. Thanks in large part to Martí's effort, the Latin American delegates got off the luxury train and faced their host. As a result, Martí writes, there is "greater recognition" and "visible respect" for Latin America, even among those in the United States who had focused on its supposed shortcomings. The delegates from Argentina, wined and dined by the business elite, stood up to say that they had no interest in "artifacts from the North" when the North closed its doors to Argentinean products. The conference in Washington might have spelled disaster for the Latin American nations, the reigns of their economies and ultimately their sovereignty handed over to an eager United States. It might have been, Martí writes for *La Nación*, on May 9, 1890, "the humiliating and definitive submission of a family of free republics, more or less confident, to a frightening and indifferent power, with a colossal appetite and with different objectives." Instead, because of Martí's cry from the heart and his judicious warnings, the congress has been "the prelude to a great concord" (la antesala de una gran concordia) (6:80).

Martí knew that all the wining and dining of the Latin delegates to the Pan-American Congress and all the after-dinner speeches about harmonious trade agreements were part of a grand performance. He suspected that even if Blaine himself faltered, which he did, the United States would be the Juggernaut of the century to come, yet Martí also insisted on presenting a united front that might deflect the impact of some policies or defer the consequences of others. In his more private writings, Martí expresses his anguish at what he witnessed in Washington, but in his official declarations, he chose to evoke the possibility of a future accord between the North and its southern neighbors.

Of course, for Martí, there was a good deal more at stake than the possibility of influencing the policies of United States toward Latin America. As always, his main concern was the future of Cuba. In his official reports on the congress Martí could not discuss the topic of Cuba, much less his plans to lead a war of insurgency against Spain, whose agents in the United States were watching his every move. However, in his letters and poems, the question of Cuba takes center stage. Martí's feelings are best expressed in the letters he wrote Gonzalo de Quesada, his protégé and ally. In a letter dated November 16, 1889, referring to the congress in Washington, Martí wrote Quesada, "All around me I see so much ugliness of spirit that I am tempted to thank you just for being the way you are" (Tanta fealdad de alma estoy viendo a mi alrededor, que me siento tentado a darle gracias por ser Ud. como es) (6:122). There are some who have already been bought, he tells Quesada, and those who, like a herd of sheep, break ranks as soon as "they see that a plate is set for them." He laments the lack of funds to carry on his plans and asks Quesada for a contribution of five dollars a month, for six months, to support a new journal, dedicated to the cause of Cuba. Martí was probably referring to *Patria*, which was eventually founded on March 14, 1892, and that became the official organ of the Cuban Revolutionary Party. Martí edited the paper until his death, assisted by Gonzalo de Quesada and Sotero Figueroa, Martí's Puerto Rican friend and collaborator, who edited the paper during Martí's frequent absences from New York.

In another letter to Quesada, written the following month, December 1889, Martí spells out his fears about Cuba's future. There is "another plan, dark and malevolent, threatening our land." It is a plan, Martí tells Quesada, to force the island into war "in order to use that as a pretext to intervene in it, and to use the role of mediator or warrantor in order to keep it" (para tener pretexto de intervenir en ella, y con el crédito de mediador, y de garantizador, quedarse con ella) (6:128). Martí saw the revival of "Clay's dream" to turn Cuba into a colony of the United States lurking behind the rhetoric of hemispheric alliance and "brotherhood" at the congress in Washington. "There is nothing more cowardly in the annals of free people: nor is there a more cold-hearted wickedness" (Cosa más cobarde no hay en los anales de los pueblos libres: Ni maldad más fría), he wrote Quesada (6:128). What is worse, there were Cubans who served those interests, under cover of a hypocritical patriotism. Those were the facts, and the solution was constant vigilance and the search for those "who might take pity on us."

In the prologue to his *Versos sencillos* (simple verses), published in New York in 1891, Martí refers to the events that were taking place in Washington. He dedicated the slim volume to two great friends and political allies, Manuel Mercado, from Mexico, and Uruguayan Enrique Estrázulas. In the prologue to his famous *Verses*, Martí refers to the agony he felt until he was certain that the Latin American nations would not readily approve the plans of the United States. It was then, he writes, that he was able to "confirm the caution and the spirit of our Latin American nations." He also writes of "the horror and shame I felt at the legitimate fear that we Cubans, with parricidal hands, might aid in the foolish plan to separate Cuba from the nations that claim it," that is, from Latin America.

There is no more compact, more brilliant vision of Latin America's history and destiny than Martí's "Our America," first published in Mexico's *El Partido Liberal*, on January 30, 1891. The essay was one of many Martí wrote during the months of the Pan-American Congress in Washington, but it stands out for its vision of Latin American history, its grasp of intercontinental politics, its wisdom and its generosity of spirit. The essay has often been read in light of Martí's indignation at the indifference of the United States toward the cause of Cuban independence. "Our America" also reveals Martí's disgust with the shameless scheming of politicians like Blaine to take over Cuba, a first step in a mighty push for absolute control of the hemisphere. This has certainly been a valid, if now obvious, reading, but "Our America" is also a treatise on good government and on the values of a wise, tolerant and compassionate individual vision.

In "Our America," Martí's message is firmly grounded on the politics of the moment, but it is also aimed far beyond the circumstances in which he labored. In some ways, the message of "Our America" extends even beyond our own contemporary parochial interests, polarized around differences that only seem irreconcilable to our own shortsightedness.

For Martí, Cuban independence was not merely a goal but a first step. It was the necessary first step that would allow a free republic to join a community of nations, indeed, to be a part of an American common market that would include the United States, not as a new master but as partner and ally. Despite his energetic advocacy for the cause of Cuban independence, Martí was not a nationalist in the narrow sense of the term. "Our America" begins with a rejection of narrow-minded regionalism, centered on the image of a "conceited villager" who thinks that "his village is the whole world." As long as he is the mayor, his rival checked and his wallet fat, the narrow-minded villager believes that "the

universal order is good." Those who cannot see beyond their own village, or their own nation, will be crushed by "giants with seven-league
boots." It has often been pointed out that the "giant" refers to the
United States, eager to divide and conquer the weak Latin American
republics. Indeed, but Martí's villager is also blind to "the battle of the
comets in the heavens," that is, ignorant of a universal order that
demands that we look up in reverence, a greater order that we ignore at
our own peril. Martí does not separate earthly politics from this transcendental vision, which distinguishes "Our America" from the crowded
archive of anti-imperialist tracts.

"Our America" is a call-to-arms, but Martí, who was raising every
dime he could find to buy arms for an eventual invasion of Cuba, does
not refer only to guns and artillery. He writes of "weapons of the mind,
which conquer all others. Trenches of ideas are worth more than
trenches of stone" (6:15). Martí's idealism is a recurring topic in biographies and eulogies. Behind the obvious praise of Martí's "idealism,"
there is often more than a hint of apology, and not a little condescen-
sion, for Martí's optimistic vision of the human condition, as if only
someone with his head in the clouds could hope for just policies and a
decent government to carry them out. It is a common, unfair misread-
ing of Martí's wisdom, which is grounded on the political realities of his
time and at the same time looks beyond them with confidence and
energy. Martí does say that ideas are ultimately stronger than weapons,
but he goes on to explain that an exclusive dependence on brute force,
though perhaps successful in the short run, will ultimately destroy both
victim and executioner.

Regional disputes must be laid aside in favor of a more inclusive, more
powerful solidarity, Martí argues. He warns against local rivalries and
against envy. There are those who raise their fists, like jealous brothers,
he writes, envious of the other's larger house, greedy for his land. In fact,
they should join their hands, so that they may become one. Martí contrasts a tradition of conflict among Latin American nations with images
of unity. "As a people," he writes, in a characteristic metaphoric flurry,
"we can no longer afford to be like the leaves of a tree, its top heavy with
flowers, way up in the air, crackling or humming this way and that, at
the whim of the sun, or buffeted and tossed by the storm. The trees
must line up to keep out the giant with seven-league boots!" (6:15).

In other words, a nation with its head in the clouds, disconnected
from its own reality, torn by petty conflicts with its neighbors, will be
easy prey to outside forces, be they political, economic or cultural. Once
the image of the giant with the seven league boots is established, Martí
does not dwell on the qualities of a potential enemy, but turns instead to

the problems that have burdened the Latin nations. With characteristic candor, Martí addresses the treatment of the native populations in the Americas. He writes with disdain of the shame that some feel because they are descendants of native people.

It should be pointed out that Martí published "Our America" in a Mexican journal, during the dictatorship of Porfirio Díaz, who surrounded himself with social "scientists" determined to modernize the country, and who was notoriously contemptuous of native people. In his provocative arguments, Martí rejects shame at a native ancestry and affirms pride in one's own history. He criticizes the mistreatment of the native populations and at the same time attacks an economic system that for centuries had grown fat on their suffering. There are those, he writes, who "curse the womb that carried them" and live abroad, away from the toil of their own mother, turning their back on her in shame because "she wears an Indian frock." The sentimental image of the abandoned mother has a concrete referent in an economy of exploitation familiar to all Latin Americans. North America, Martí writes, "is drowning its Indians in their own blood," but "our America" must find a way to embrace them. In 1910, almost twenty years after Martí published "Our America" in Mexico, Porfirio Díaz was forced into exile, while Emiliano Zapata led his native guerrillas against the haciendas of Morelos and Guerrero.

From a sense of shame, Martí writes, we must move to the confidence of pride, not the false pride of the villager but the pride of commitment and solidarity. Martí appeals strongly to a sense of Latin pride as the foundation on which to build a progressive future. Martí proposes a manual for conducting ourselves and for governing our Latin nations, so distinct, so promising, so recently created from such disparate elements. Martí's recommendation is simple and straightforward: "A government is born from the nation itself. The spirit of that government must reflect the spirit of the nation" (6:17). Martí warns against the facile imitation of foreign models, yet his outlook remains consistently cosmopolitan. He preferred the dynamic tension of paradox to the rigidity of predictable polarities. He admired many traditions and drew from the best of them liberally, assimilating and translating. A homegrown imitator of French manners and fashions would turn into a harmless, if somewhat ridiculous, provincial dandy, but when people abandon their roots for a poor imitation of foreign models, disaster is sure to follow.

In Martí's America, "the imported book" must be vanquished by "natural man." Martí admired democracy above all other systems of government, but a democracy could not be grafted on to a country without regard for its history and for its own political realities. "Our

America" is a manual of good government, based on a series of contrasts
between what is "natural" and what is "artificial"; in other words, what
is organic, alive and evolving and what is stilted, specious and stagnant.
Without this grounding on "Nature," in the Emersonian sense, a system
of government, even one developed by individuals with the best intentions, stands on shaky ground.

In Emerson's writings, Martí learned that the individual must define
his or her own path. In his meditation on the future of "our America,"
he takes Emerson's faith in the power of the individual and expands it to
suggest ways to govern wisely. Martí insisted that each nation must
develop a vital, dynamic form of government, grounded on its own past
and its own circumstances, its course set for a future where the rights of
all would be protected. Martí did not see his plan as a mere possibility
for a distant future. He was convinced that to consider the needs of all
was not idealistic but rather politically wise. In other words, in the long
run, it made sense to found a system on the needs of all rather than on
the whims of a few. Any other system was headed for instability and
chaos. When those who govern willfully or unwittingly ignore "the true
elements of a nation," the result is tyranny.

In "Our America" Martí contrasts two different versions of what con-
stitutes "culture." In Latin America, the Creole elite associated "culture" with the knowledge and products of Europe, what Martí calls "the
European book." The Pan-American Congress in Washington was
designed in part to display the appeal of a new "book," the prototype of
"the American way of life," newly minted and ready for export, full
steam ahead. In the congress, American businessmen and their allies in
Washington were eager to present the United States not only as a new
partner but as a model nation for the Latin American republics. As Martí
saw it, in order to deal with its powerful neighbor, the nations of Latin
America would have to rethink their own ideas about what constituted
culture. What Martí calls the "uncultured element" of a nation would
rebel against oppression by any means at hand, including violence. It was
necessary to educate those who would govern in order to create leaders
capable of understanding the needs of all people.

Echoing the progressive thinkers of his day, Martí argued that the
great leveler in a democracy is education. Throughout his writings, he
sets forth an educational program to bring "the uncultured element" to
the level of civic participation. "The young," he writes, "go out to make
their way in the world wearing Yankee or French spectacles, hoping to
govern a people they do not know . . .. To know one's country and to
govern it according to that knowledge is the only way to free it from
tyranny" (6:17–18). Martí's comments on curriculum, radical by the

standards of his day, still resonate in contemporary debates about literacy and canon formation. Martí tells all future leaders to learn about the histories of their own people. "The history of America," he writes, "from the Incas to the present, must be taught to the letter, even if the history of the rulers of Greece is overlooked." Martí returns time and again to the theme of pride in "our long-suffering American republics."

Implicit in Martí's plea for political solidarity is a radical call to cultural unity throughout the Americas, a message that resonates throughout the twentieth century. Unity, it must be added, did not mean the erasure of difference for the sake of an ideal nation, powerful and monolithic. In Martí's vision unity does not contradict plurality. Martí had learned first-hand that in the United States racism and exclusion were destroying this sacred tenet of democracy, unity in plurality. In his writings about the process of nation building, Martí hoped to recapture a spirit of solidarity where distinct identities would inhabit the same sphere and thus unleash the power to transform societies in positive ways. Martí's faith in the possibility of human cooperation has nothing to do with the noisy patriotism of "my country right or wrong," or with the rhetoric of harmony that flowed so easily from the lips of every other politician. It is rather pride based on knowledge of the past, its glories and its horrors, and on hope not only for the achievement of personal goals but for the building of a better world.

In "Our America" Martí presents a compact reconstruction of the history of the Latin American nations. In 1810, in a Mexican village, "a priest, a few lieutenants, and a woman" unleashed the pent-up fury that would lead to Mexico's independence from Spain. The priest was Miguel Hidalgo, whose gave the *grito de Dolores*, the battle cry of Mexican independence. September 16, the day Hidalgo turned his parishioners into fighters, is celebrated today as Mexico's Independence Day. One of Hidalgo's lieutenants was José María Morelos, a skillful guerrilla leader who gained control of southern Mexico until Spanish forces captured him and executed him in December, 1815. The woman Martí mentions was Josefa Ortiz, the wife of a Spanish magistrate who sided with the insurgents and was sentenced to prison.

In one of the most difficult passages of "Our America," bristling with metaphors, Martí explains why the righteous fury of the first independence movements and the sacrifice and heroism of its leaders failed to produce democratic republics. In times of peace, he writes, "heroism is more scarce, because it is less glorious than it is during times of war." "It is easier," he goes on, "to die with honor than to think with logic." After the battle is won, it is difficult to unite "divisive, arrogant, exotic or ambitious beliefs" (6:18). Generations of leaders, scholars and historians have debated the points that Martí so lucidly raises. Despite the success of various independence movements, the colonial legacy of Latin America endured in political systems and social structures that failed to build truly democratic republics.

In Latin America, the revolutionary struggles against the foreign oppressor triumphed because their energy came from *el alma de la tierra*, the soul of the nation, in fact, the soul of the land itself and the very soil we stand on. When that "soul" is betrayed by bookish leaders, disdainful of native cultures and infatuated with foreign formulas, the result is the same old oppression with a different mask. The new governments become the unwitting heirs of the colonizer's systems of oppressions, and reforms fail when they are not anchored in "local realities."

Martí writes of a continent "disjointed" after three centuries under a system that denied human beings the use of their reason to determine their own fate. New systems emerged that ignored the very people who had helped bring them to power: the dispossessed, the unlettered, the underdogs. The new governments demanded that people incapable of reading or signing their name become citizens in a republic based on reason: the reason of all citizens, "not the university reason of the few held over the country reason of the others." In a nutshell, "the problem of independence did not require a change of forms but a change of spirit" (6:19). The great tradition of individual rights, anchored on the power of reason, was not enough to create new democratic republics. What was needed was a new kind of reason, grounded on local realities, not beholden to imported categories, and above all, enlightened by understanding and compassion.

A republic might call itself a democracy and dutifully go through its civic rituals, but without Martí's "change of spirit," oppression would return, just as "the tiger, scared off by gun fire, returns at night to find its prey." "The colony lived on in the republic," and our America must save itself from its past mistakes, "the arrogance of its capital cities, the short-lived victories of its scorned peasantry, the excessive importation of foreign formulas and ideas, the wicked, politically unwise disdain for the aboriginal race." "The tiger waits, behind every tree, crouching at every corner. It will die, with its paws up in the air, spewing flames from its eyes"; yet "these countries will be saved" through the spirit of moderation, through harmony with Nature, and through a change of spirit in each individual (6:19).

In a final flourish, Martí recaps his arguments about the history and the future of "our America." In what is perhaps the most brilliant political passage he ever wrote, Martí creates a portrait of Latin America through the image of a single body composed of conflicting fragments, held together by the power of love. "We were a vision," he writes, "with the chest of an athlete, the hands of a dandy and the face of a child. We were a mask, with breeches from England, a Parisian vest, a North American jacket, and the cap of a Spanish hunter." From the shreds of the many cultures that foundered on the shores of our America, Martí's inclusive "we" is united in a single image. From this hybrid image others arise that complement it and contradict it at once: the Indian, the Negro, the peasant, the disenfranchised and dispossessed. Martí writes: "The Indian circled around us in silence, and went to the mountain-top to baptize his children. The Negro, spied from afar, sang in the night the music of his heart, alone and unrecognized, among the waves and the wild animals. The campesino, the creator, revolted in blind indignation against the disdainful city, which he had helped to create" (6:20).

Martí's image coalesces fleetingly into a recognizable whole only to shatter into fragments, as if pulled apart by forces that destroy all sense of harmony. Yet even as he paints a shattered image, Martí suggests a sense of beauty, hope and unity, atoms of energy that coalesce from dispersion itself. It is that spark that then rekindles the hope of what might be. Martí continues to build on the metaphor of clothing to suggest the conflicting elements that have made up our America. We came into the world with sandals on our feet and a headband around our head, and ended up wearing the professor's gown and the soldier's epaulets, he writes. It would have taken a genius to unite these disparate elements, "to bring together, with love in our hearts and with the daring of the founders, the native headband and the professor's gown." In other words, the mark of genius would have been to bring together native wisdom and European knowledge and "to open up possibilities for the Indian; to make a place for the able Negro; to fit liberty to the body of those who fought and vanquished for her sake" (6:20). Martí represents our America as a fragmented body wearing a costume made up of disparate pieces, poorly suited to the body it was meant to clothe and protect. The failures of the past, however, need not be repeated in the future. The work of genius, that is, the work of the future, lies in the remaking of that garment so that it does fit the entire body of the republic, so that it warms and protects.

From the old masters, Spain and the European powers that planted their standards on America's coast, we inherited a system that empowered some at the expense of others. We are heirs to "the judge, the general, the scholar and the idle landowner." Young people rose against the old system, only to fall back in sterile glory. The common people "pushed away the golden staffs of the oppressors and became blinded by their own victories." Martí refers to early independence movements that ended in failure and suggests a different path not only for Cuba for all the Latin American nations. When Martí writes, "[n]either the European book, nor the Yankee book, contained the key to the Spanish American enigma" (6:20), it goes without saying that the "key" is in our own backyard, and we must find it.

Time and again, Martí refers to our America's violent past and contrasts it with a hopeful future. "We have tried hate," he writes, "and our nations went from bad to worse." We have been exhausted by "useless hatred." We are weary of the old conflict between the pen and the sword, between reason and faith, "between the city and the country, weary of the impossible and divisive rule of urban castes over the natural nation, tempestuous and inert." Now we begin, tentatively, without knowing why, "to try love": "Se empieza, como sin saberlo, a probar el amor" (6:20).

The Pan-American Congress in Washington was staged like a festival of nations, with all the pomp and ceremony of the international expositions that had flourished during the second half of the nineteenth century. Martí saw through the pageantry, and what he saw caused him untold anguish, so much that he became sick and had to retreat to the countryside of upstate New York. One of the grand emblems of the congress in Washington was especially troubling. It was a coat of arms with an image of the eagle of the United States, clutching in its claws the flags of all the Latin nations. The emblem was supposed to represent unity, but to Martí it represented the true spirit of the congress: the United States in control of all its neighboring nations, and perhaps Cuba's independence lost in a ruthless grab for control of the Western hemisphere. It is all the more remarkable that, against such odds, Martí found a kernel of hope in the coming together of all nations. Many of the Latin delegates listened to his warnings and refused to endorse Blaine's plans for arbitration in the affairs of the Latin American republics. Their vote against the role of the United States as the "perpetual tutor" of the Latin nations was a blow to Blaine's power (6:100).

In his essays for *La Nación*, Martí summarizes the diversity of opinions about the Pan-American Congress that he found in North American newspapers. In the American press, Martí learned that support for Blaine's project for the aggressive expansion of U.S. influence among its neighbors was far from unanimous. The *New York Times* wrote disparagingly of "The Blaine Myth," arguing that Blaine "takes a peculiarly shallow and un-American view of the transactions in which he is engaged," going so far as to call him a "bully" in his dealings with "our neighbors to the south" (October 9, 1889:4). During the months he participated in the Pan-American Congress, Martí appealed not only to the Latin nations but to the leaders and the people of the United States who might be more inclined to support genuine hemispheric cooperation. "While there are those ready to dazzle, to divide, to scheme, so that the rapacious eagle might tear off a piece with its beak," he writes, "there are others who are ready to deserve the trade they desire through honest dealings and through respect for the liberty of others" (6:35). Martí appealed to those in the United States whose "sensible opinion" told them that aggression would only cause harm and may indeed lead to the irreparable loss of "legitimate trade with the republics of the South."

Martí not only exposed the hypocrisy that lurked in the pageantry of the Pan-American Congress, he rewrote its script, suggesting to all people the possibility of genuine cooperation, based on mutual respect and on a radical definition of love. For Martí *amor* and *caridad* are interchangeable. Both terms, love and charity, have a common denominator: reverence for the natural world and compassion for all beings, a revolutionary force indeed.

Martí saw what this force might accomplish among the nations of the Americas, when "people stand up and greet one another," when they ask each other, "What are we like?" The first step towards cooperation on any front, commercial, cultural or political, must be this fundamental question, founded on a desire to know and learn from the other. The youth of the Americas must understand that "there is too much imitation, and that salvation lies in our ability to create" (6:20). True freedom cannot be limited to the liberation of the self but must be expansive and inclusive: "If it is to be viable, freedom must be sincere and complete. If a republic does not open its arms to all and prosper with all, the republic dies" (6:20–21). "Strategy and politics are one and the same," Martí writes. He lays out strategies for survival and prosperity in an atmosphere of creative criticism, for "criticism is healthy, when our hearts and our minds are united." A republic prospers when its leaders read from the book of nature, when they read to apply their knowledge, not to imitate what others have done. Cultural independence follows economic and political autonomy: "Playwrights bring native characters to the stage. Academics discuss viable topics. . . . In the Indian republics, leaders learn Indian" (6:21).

Martí believed that the republics of our America would overcome all dangers but not before they faced what threatened to divide them from the inside and what threatened to destroy them from the outside. Characteristically, as his essay draws to a close, Martí restates the problems in order to suggest creative solutions. Throughout "Our America,"

Martí calls for homegrown wisdom rather than borrowed knowledge; he warns of the shortsighted arrogance of the city against the country, the grotesque legacy of centuries of colonialism. He urges leaders to be inclusive and fair in their vision for their nation. He ends by returning to a constant topic in his writings: race and racism. Racism directed at the native populations would be the ruin of what he called "the Indian republics." Racism directed at people of African descents would ruin the rest.

Martí was the first in our America, and perhaps in any continent, to put symbolic quotations around the word "race." While he recognizes evident differences among all human beings, he also knew that "bookstore races," at odds with "the justice of Nature," had been created to divide people. Time and again, he affirms that "the soul, equal and eternal, emanates from bodies that are diverse in shape and color" (El alma emana, igual y eterna, de los cuerpos diversos en forma y en color) (6:22). True freedom is inseparable from respect for all those bodies, not just some of them, and only those nations that could transform this simple fact into a guiding vision would survive and prosper.

Throughout his essays, Martí looks for ways to turn the tables on the United States, calling it "the other America." Privately Martí expressed his anguish over the increasing power of the United States in Latin American affairs. In the political arena of the late nineteenth century, plans to make Cuba a colony of the United States or even a new state had been revived, though support for such plans was far from unanimous. In his private writings, Martí expressed his anguish, justified and prophetic as it turned out, over the threat to Cuba's independence. In "Our America" and other essays relating to the Pan-American Congress, he followed a different strategy. While exposing the danger posed by the United States, often in highly metaphoric, allusive language, he chose not to demonize the enemy, for such a move would only feed its power.

Martí knew that despite its rhetoric of intercontinental harmony, the congress in Washington was part of a grand plan to control Latin American markets, and perhaps gain Cuba and Puerto Rico in the process. "Our America" concludes with an appeal to those North Americans who might be persuaded to support a fair partnership with the Latin nations, and also support or at least not oppose the cause of Cuban independence. The Pan-American Congress, whatever the intentions of its organizers, had the virtue of representing the Latin American republics in a new light. As Martí saw it, the work of the Latin American delegates in Washington countered stereotypes about "hot-headed Latins" in need of a friendly sheriff to oversee them or about illiterate hordes in need of a strong leader, with strings firmly attached to the State Department.

Martí refers to the United States as "an enterprising and vigorous people," who disdain our America because they know so little about us: "The disdain of our formidable neighbor, who does not know us, is the greatest danger facing our America. As the day of the visit draws near, it is urgent that our neighbor know our America, and know her soon, so that it will not disdain her. Out of ignorance, perhaps, it might begin to covet her. Yet out of respect, once it knows her, it might withdraw its hands" (6:22). Martí knew that the day of "the visit" by the United States to the islands of the Caribbean was near. In the face of it, he hoped that the United States would realize that in the long run its best interests would not be served by controlling the affairs of Latin America or by taking over Cuba and Puerto Rico once Spain had been driven out. In 1898, three years after Martí's death in Dos Ríos, the day of the dreaded visit arrived, and the struggle for independence was transformed almost overnight into the Spanish-American war, a war between a former superpower and the youthful heir to the title.

Perhaps Martí foresaw the outcome of the so-called Spanish-American war, yet he also knew that defeats and victories, whatever their actual appearance, are seldom unequivocal and that the vanquished may one day thrive in the ruins abandoned by the victors. Martí insisted that it would be narrow-minded and provincial to attribute "a fatal congenital wickedness to the continent's fair-skinned nation simply because it does not speak our language, or see our home as we see it, or because its political flaws are so unlike ours" (6:22). In "Our America" Martí spells out the flaws he has seen in the United States, while at the same time warning that we must try to look beyond them. He believed that a way could be found to deal wisely with a powerful neighbor, even one who never thought "highly of a querulous, dark-complexioned people," and who did not look kindly on those who, "though less favored by history," still struggle to become free nations.

In the final paragraph of "Our America," Martí decisively rejects racial categories as false and divisive, yet he ends the essay with a contrast between the "fair-skinned" people of the continent, "el pueblo rubio del continente," and the darker folk, "trigueños," to the south. The formula is deliberately simplistic.

Still, Martí concludes his call to Latin solidarity with an emphasis on "racial" differences between northern and southern hemispheres. The decision to underscore such differences, even if he has just called them artificial and divisive, is tactical. Martí had seen firsthand the centrality of race and the persistence of race-hatred in the politics and culture of the United States. Moreover, he knew that prejudices based on racial and cultural differences figured prominently in discussions about the role of the United States in Latin America. For the benefit of his Latin readers, especially those dazzled by the might of the United States and impressed by its unquestionable energy, he wanted to lay the cards on the table, the better to suggest what an alliance with the United States might bring with it.

"Our America" opens with an image of a narrow-minded, "conceited villager," self-important, certain of standing at the center of the universe, and blind to what lies beyond the town walls. The essay concludes with a mythological image of a flying sower, whose vision encompasses the entire continent, unifying and planting new seeds: "From the Río Grande to the Straits of Magellan, the Great Semí, astride the condor, over the romantic nations of the continent and the sorrowful islands of the sea, sowed the seeds of the new America" (6:23). In Martí's essay, we begin in a village and end in the cosmos. Its first character is a villager; its last is a mythic traveler, a sower and a seer, a harbinger of the future. For Martí, any political strategy must be informed by the possibility of such a journey, or it becomes a dead letter, the recycled rhetoric of a small town politico at the local ballpark.

The delegates to the Pan-American Congress in Washington and Martí's readers in the United States and in Latin America got the message. The great luxury train put at the service of the visiting dignitaries continued its swift journey through the American heartland. However, as the hard realities of the congress became clearer, thanks in large part to Martí's efforts, more and more Latin delegates stayed in Washington. Others left the train along its route and made their own way back to the capital, traveling at their own expense, "their collars up around their ears, a three-day old beard on their face," sadder and wiser, one might add (6:107). By the time the train left Richmond, the final stop before Washington, it was empty.

CHAPTER 5

BILINGUAL EMERSON

References to Ralph Waldo Emerson (1803–1882) appear throughout Martí's writings, in articles, reviews and letters. In one of Martí's epistolary articles for the Caracas newspaper *La Opinión Nacional* (national opinion), published on October 1, 1881, Martí refers to Emerson's "natural philosophy," perhaps his earliest reference to the author of *Nature* (9:49). The following year, within days of Emerson's death, Martí wrote a long essay simply titled "Emerson." It was also published in *La Opinión Nacional*, on May 19, 1882. The essay "Emerson" has been frequently anthologized and is the undisputed centerpiece of any discussion of Martí's indebtedness to the famous New Englander. And yet, among Martí's many references to Emerson, there is the intriguing phrase "The evening of Emerson" (la tarde de Emerson), a privileged moment "when man loses his sense of self and is transfused into the world" (cuando pierde el hombre el sentido de sí y se trasfunde en el mundo) (21:387). Through the canonical essay and the rather orphaned fragment, I want to review, if not answer, questions that are central to Martí's worldview and to his debt to Emerson: What is the sense of this loss of self? What is meant by a "transfusion" into the world? *Trasfundir* or *transfundir:* to transfuse; to pour from one vessel to another.

In his elegiac essay Martí summarizes, translates, glosses and appropriates Emerson, creating in the end something entirely original, not only a new text but also a blueprint for living and dying. "Ingesting" might be a better term, for there is something organic, rather than strictly intellectual, about Martí's appropriation of Emerson. José Ballón has written that in his appropriation of Emerson, Martí produced a "common bilingual ocean" or a "bilingual web" (54). This "web" and the intense intellectual labor it represents are the necessary precursors for the loss of self and the "transfusion" into the world recorded in Martí's *War Diaries*, the last words he ever wrote.

In "Emerson" Martí translates and paraphrases fragments from Emerson's works, weaving them into an image of the dead writer that is also a kind of self-portrait. The task of determining the exact source of Martí's appropriations of Emerson remains incomplete, for it is impossible at times to tell where Emerson ends and Martí begins. Moreover, an exhaustive account of Martí's references and allusions to Emerson would not explain his elusive aura in Martí's writings and in the way he conducted his life. It is not simply a matter of quotation, but of incorporation of another's writings in order to produce what is neither a copy nor an original but something new, a truly Emersonian product, Martí's own "revelation" not "the history of theirs."

In *Individualism and its Discontents: Appropriations of Emerson 1880–1950*, Charles Mitchell explains that the genteel American critics of the late nineteenth century transformed Emerson into an icon of homegrown virtues, a sweet reminder of another era, superseded as the onslaught of modernity altered the cultural and political landscape. Martí had little use for New England virtues pickled for the consumption of undergraduates. He took Emerson's insights and used them to help define his own cultural and political agenda. He took the lessons of Emerson's book into the battlefield and used them to make sense out of his own odyssey and finally to make help us make sense out of his death.

Emerson died on April 27, 1882. Martí's essay was published a month later in Caracas, in *La Opinión Nacional*, on May 19. After Emerson's death, newspapers and magazines published articles and obituaries praising Emerson, already immortalized as the "Sage of Concord." Martí's essay, however, is not simply an elegy written for the occasion, hastily sent off to satisfy the curiosity of Spanish-speaking readers.

For many years now, scholars and critics have traced references to Emerson in Martí's writings. In his account of Martí's debt to Emerson, Ballón has found remarkable examples of the many ways Martí used Emerson as a source for creating his own poetry and prose. Ballón shows, for example, a striking case of poetic intertextuality between Emerson's early poem "A Mountain Grave" and one of Martí's most famous *Versos sencillos* (simple verses). In Emerson's poem, written when he was 28 years old, the fear of death yields to the realization that death is part of nature's cycle: "Of Nature's child the common fate" (*Complete Works* 9: 390–1). Fear vanishes when death is seen as nature's embrace. Emerson's early poem begins with the question, "Why fear to die," and moves on to an almost erotic surrender to the forces of nature: "Amid great Nature's halls/ Girt in by mountain walls/ And washed with waterfalls/ It would please me to die."

Emerson wrote "A Mountain Grave" after the death of his young wife Ellen Tucker, in the winter of 1831. "With Emerson in mind," Ballón writes, Martí reflects on his own death (111). For Martí, nature is also the healer, even in death, but Martí adds a militant, almost martial, tone to his own renunciation: "I want to leave the world/ Through the natural door:/ In a cart of green leaves/ They will take me to die" (Yo quiero salir del mundo/ Por la puerta natural:/ En un carro de hojas verdes/ A morir me han de llevar.) In the next stanza, as it has so often been pointed out, Martí prophesizes his own heroic death in the battlefield: "Do not lay me in dark/ To die like a traitor: I am good, and like a good man, I will die facing the sun!" (No me pongan en lo oscuro/ A morir como un traidor: ¡Yo soy bueno, y como bueno/ Moriré de cara al sol!) (16:98).

Despite Martí's evident reliance on Emerson's vision of death, he radically transforms it. In Emerson's poem, there is identification with Nature, Ballón writes, through "a subject that is static and cloistered" ("Amid great Nature's halls/Girt by mountain walls"). On the other hand, Martí's poetic persona is dynamic and expansive. Emerson's "walls" become Martí's "natural door," and death is part of an ongoing change rather than a state to be achieved. In Martí's brief verses, the decay of the flesh yields to the triumph of vegetable matter, so that "the physical organism does not die but rather germinates" (Ballón 113). According to Ballón, Martí's poem has preserved "the vegetable frame" of Emerson's "A Mountain Grave," but he has added a communal element. As it does in Emerson, in Martí's poem death means intimacy with nature, but in the Cuban's verses, death also becomes a civic occasion, attracting those others who have come to bury and also to witness the poet-hero's passage into a new light.

If there is enclosure and stasis in Emerson's early poem of mourning, what critic Harold Bloom has called "the power at the crossing" is evident in Emerson's essays and in his journal. According to Bloom, Emerson valued transition, the flight from "our God of tradition" and "our God of rhetoric" to a "God [who] may fire the heart with his presence" (Bloom 322). In Emerson there is "power at the crossing," "because power for him resided only at the crossing, at the actual moment of transition" (ibid.). Martí opened himself to such a possibility. Defeat only served to rekindle his energies. For him, the poet's passage into a new reality came not through the writing of a new poem but through the final experience of the Cuban countryside, during the weeks before his death. Martí's diary, fragmentary by definition, contains notes of that final crossing but not its totality, which can only be imagined, the way we imagine a distant bonfire by its reddish gleam.

In Emerson's writings, Martí discovered an echo of his own faith in the transforming powers of human creativity and solidarity. Martí shared Emerson's desire, stated at the opening of *Nature*, for a "an original relation to the universe," "a poetry and philosophy of insight and not of tradition," and "a religion by revelation to us, and not the history of theirs" (*Collected Works* 1:7). In Emerson's works, individual wisdom is strengthened in the quietude that only nature can offer, but it also receives power from human contact. In his own writings and in his political activism, Martí struggled to define a similar credo. Emerson aged in the sweet retirement of Concord, while Martí worked frantically to organize a war of liberation that would have international repercussions, a struggle that would demand his own life.

Martí was more than an enthusiastic reader of Concord's famous poet-philosopher. As a poet and a political activist, Martí situated himself at the very source of an Emersonian tradition whose complexities and contradictions run through the bedrock of the culture of the United States, right up to our own time. In his writings, Martí appropriates Emerson, adapting the writer's English words to his native language, molding them to suit his own circumstances. In the United States, Martí, an outspoken disciple of Emerson, remained the quintessential outsider in a place he called the imperial city. As he dreamed of democracy for Cuba and Latin America, he witnessed the shameless corruption of democratic ideals, even as orators and politicians pontificated about their endurable worth. Martí recognized the contradiction at the core of North American culture, but he believed that we, those he called "Latin people," *la gente latina*, could move beyond it. His appropriation of Emerson stands out as an original point in our long dialogue with the politics and the culture of the United States.

As Emerson's greatness became a commonplace, the potential of his writings to move and inspire, the way they had moved and inspired Martí, was concealed in layers of misreadings, or no readings at all. The possibility that Emerson's writings might suggest ways to challenge established orthodoxies was disturbing. It was more advisable to focus on the virtuous qualities of the Sage of Concord and polish the rough edges of his complexities. The result was a version of American culture that was, in Mitchell's words, "well-mannered, polite, and politically united" (5). National unity proved to be a useful chimera, which in fact excluded everyone except the white men who manufactured it in cloistered libraries and prestigious universities.

During the celebrations of Emerson's centennial in 1903, Charles William Eliot, then president of Harvard, portrayed the Sage of

Concord as the source of democratic ideals that might survive and even thrive in the new territories acquired by the widening reach of the United States. According to Mitchell, Eliot, who was a member of the Anti-Imperialist League, was opposed to U.S. military intervention in Cuba, Puerto Rico and the Philippines. However, as an educational reformer, he also saw the opportunity to bring education "to those less developed races," Eliot's phrase. In other words, although the imperial designs of the United States troubled the white liberal elite, they thought in time there might be a silver lining. The people of Cuba, Puerto Rico and the Philippines might in fact become productive members of a new "civilization," benevolently ruled by the United States. Martí knew that Cuba's liberation from Spain would encourage the imperial designs of the United States, and "the Colossus of the North," as he called it, had nothing but contempt for the island people it set out to conquer.

According to Mitchell, articles in the *Nation* reacted to a nascent American imperialism by proclaiming Emerson as "the prophet of active dissent" (30). Emersonian individualism might justify the expansion of an aggressive young nation, right up to the New Frontier. At the same time, Emerson was considered the source of democratic values that were being violated everyday at home and abroad. At home, in the continued exclusion of women from full participation in the republic, in the lynching of African Americans; abroad, in the devastation caused by the invasions of Cuba, Puerto Rico and the Philippines.

In his chapter "Emerson: Power at the Crossing," Bloom clarifies another side of the paradox at the heart of the Emersonian tradition, which is to say at the heart of the culture of the United States. Bloom writes of Emerson as "*the* American theoretician of power—be it political, literary, spiritual, economic—because he took the risk of exalting transition for its own sake." Bloom goes on to say that he is "happier when the consequence [of the power of the Emersonian "crossing"] is Whitman's 'Crossing Brooklyn Ferry' than when the Emersonian product is the first Henry Ford, but Emerson is canny enough to prophesy both disciples. There is a great chill at the center of his cosmos, which remains ours, both the chill and the cosmos" (313). In his cheap frock coat and worn shoes, Martí felt that chill. In poetry, prose and oratory he set out to proclaim it to the four winds. In the throes of modernity, he recast the prophetic mode, crying out from a wilderness of iron and steel.

Far from the Concord fireside, in New York City, Martí felt the Emersonian chill in his bones. One of the most magnificent representations of it is in a poem titled "Amor de ciudad grande," an ambiguous phrase, usually translated as "love in a great city," or simply "love in the city," as it appears in the excellent translation included in *Selected Writings*, published in 2002. Yet "Amor de ciudad grande" also suggests an entirely different meaning: "love of the city." "Love of the Great City" is the translation given in Ramos's *Divergent Modernities* (216 n. 27). The ambiguity of Martí's title is central to the poem, where the city is finally rejected but not before one last look, or rather one last verse, describing the very horrors from which the poet flees: "The city is a cage of dead doves/ and avid hunters!" (Jaula es la villa de palomas muertas/ Y ávidos cazadores!).

As the apocalyptic vision of the city unfolds, the poet simultaneously looks and looks away, like a schizophrenic version of Lot's wife, turned into a statue of salt as punishment for a last look at Sodom and Gomorrah. There is a sense of flight throughout the poem, as if the poet, fleeing what he cannot bear to see, nonetheless looks over his shoulder for a final glimpse, spelling it out for the reader, who now must bear the burden of that vision. In "Love in the City," though cornered, the poet turns on his heels to reassert his ethical self: "I am honorable, and I am afraid!" (¡Yo soy honrado, y tengo miedo!) (16:172). In the prologue to *Versos libres* (free verses), Martí writes that *honradez*, which is both "honesty" and "integrity," is the quality he most values in poetry. A related substantive, *honra*, means "honor," so that the sense of the phrase "Yo soy honrado" is closer to "I am a man of honor." In any case, in matters of honor, "honorable" in English sounds a little stuffy and certainly judicial, where as "honrado" rings with the genuine pathos of someone who is trying to maintain his integrity in a crooked city, and is afraid: "y tengo miedo."

In his essay on "Love in the City," González-Echevarría takes the question of honor a step further by defining *honradez* as "fidelity of the word to the act of will that creates it in the world," an act that makes "word" and "act" inseparable (164). This inseparability, or rather the desire for it, is at the core of Martí's poetics, sketchily outline in the prologue to *Versos libres*. The "disharmonious counterpoint," González-Echevarría's phrase, in "Love in the City" appropriates the Romantic tradition and recasts it in the chaotic city. If the modern city has crushed the sweet poetry of nostalgia, poetry, or in broader terms, the act of writing itself, imposes a fleeting order on its chaos.

Imposing order on chaos through an act of creative will is an arduous process that all but destroys the self, metaphorically recast in the poem as a "startled hare" fleeing the hunter. The poem overcomes its own impasse by looking to the future, to a different resolution that would generate a new kind of language, to a reconstruction "with the remnants of tradition," useful in the "social regeneration he envisioned for Cuba, Puerto Rico and Latin America" (Schulman, "Void and renewal" 161). Through the ordeal of suffering, the "wall" separating word and act, and the poet from freedom and vision, may break down: "I have not yet suffered enough to break down the wall that separates me, oh pain!, from my vineyard!" ('¡No he padecido/ Bastante aún, para romper el muro/ Que me aparta ¡oh dolor! De mi viñedo!') (16:172). The breaking down of this symbolic wall will come when Martí arrives in his "vineyard," the backwoods of Cuba, where, on the eve of death, word and action find their common ground.

In the city of Martí's poem, people "make love in the streets, standing up, in the dust of saloons and public squares" ('Se ama de pie, en las calles, entre el polvo/ De los salones y las plazas') (16:170). When bodies are torn, their insides look like "crushed fruits." This is not Emerson's sweet return to Nature, but it is Martí's discovery of his own "nature" at the heart of "an age of parched lips, of sleepless nights, of life crushed before its time." It is a city where "Bodies are nothing now but trash, and pits, and tatters" ('¡No son los cuerpos ya sino desechos,/Y fosas, y jirones!') This is a poetry not of exalted souls but of broken bodies, and broken hopes, rescued nonetheless in a final affirmation of an ethical self: *soy honrado*. In "Love in the City," as in many of the poems of *Versos libres*, Martí is as close to Baudelaire as he is to Emerson.

Martí was aware of the radical nature of his poetry. In a comment on a book recounting "the all too peaceful life of William Cullen Bryant," published in *La Nación* in June of 1883, Martí alludes to his own work and to his own not at all peaceful life. He writes that Bryant "was a poet, a white poet, in the comfortable manner of Wordsworth, not like those others, unfortunate and glorious, who feed on their own entrails" (fue poeta, blanco poeta, al modo cómodo de Wordsworth, no como aquellos otros infortunados y gloriosos, que se alimentan de sus mismas entrañas) (9:413). "Love in the City" is the representation of a sort of autocannibalism, "feeding on your own entrails," a gutting of the self for the sake of poetic vision.

Martí feared that, in the struggle for the soul of a nation, greed was defeating love, commerce was smothering poetry, and he feared the consequences for Cuba, Puerto Rico and Latin America. Yet as a radical democrat and an unrepentant optimist, he would accept neither the chill nor the cosmos as the final word. Martí wanted nothing more than to lay the foundations of a revolutionary legacy, one capable of transforming individuals and through them, the world we live in.

Martí read Emerson not as a genteel sage but as a radical thinker. He translated, glossed and appropriated Emerson, fusing his words into his own writing as part of a revolutionary blue print. In "Self-Reliance" Emerson writes, "[i]n every work of genius we recognize our own rejected thoughts; they come back to us with a certain alienated majesty. Great works of art have no more affecting lesson for us than this" (*Collected Works* 2:27). In the writings of Emerson, Martí recognized his own "rejected thoughts," and he found in Emerson what was already his. Martí's original reading of Emerson invites us to find other links that may add to our understanding of his unique position as an exile in New York. Martí would have seen through the many versions of Emerson, used and abused by admirers and critics alike. The question was to lay claim to a tradition that would lead to liberation and enlightenment under whatever names they might appear.

Martí's situation as an exile and a reader of the American tradition may be compared to the very different yet analogous position of African American educator, civil rights leader and cultural critic W. E. B. Du Bois (1868–1963). For Du Bois, the question was not to read or misread Emerson but rather to rewrite him in a new image. The work of Du Bois offers a suggestive counterpoint to Martí's own appropriation of an Emersonian tradition. During Martí's years in New York, 1880 through 1895, Du Bois was an undergraduate at Fisk University. From 1888 to 1895, he was a student at Harvard, where he studied philosophy with William James. In 1895, the year of Martí's death, Du Bois became the first African American to receive a Ph.D. at Harvard University. To my knowledge, Martí and Du Bois never crossed paths, yet for several years they lived in the same region of the United States, a fact that is altogether inconsequential and yet suggests a tantalizing scenario: an imaginary dialogue between these two men.

In 1868, the year Du Bois was born, Martí was 15 years old. Two years later he was condemned to six years in prison for his activities against Spain. Martí was forced to live in exile most of his life, while Du Bois chose to die in it, as a citizen of Ghana. Such parallels are suggestive because, in spite of the obvious differences in their lives, Du Bois and Martí were radical democrats at a time when the ideals of democracy were being eroded on many fronts.

Like Martí, Du Bois came to believe that it was either naïve or cynical to think that the sacred declaration "all men are created equal" was a self-evident truth in the country that was founded on such a lofty ideal. They believed that a democratic republic worthy of the name faced the formidable task of creating a level field where all people may have the same opportunity to build their own lives and to carry their individual potential to its complete fruition. For Du Bois and Martí, this belief in a radical democracy lay at the core of everything they fought for. Du Bois battled in a country divided by a "color line" that was often a bloody trench. Martí fought against tyranny in Cuba even as he battled prejudice and race-hatred in the ranks of his own supporters.

Both Du Bois and Martí believed that the real measure of progress was to be found in our ability to move toward true equality among all human beings. At the end of the nineteenth century, human achievements in the arts and the sciences were evident, but without a plan for true equality, such achievements would have a limited impact. Two people, miles away apart, could talk to each other through a wire. The old steam engine would be replaced by a sleek new model. From conquering the frontier, we might set out to conquer outer space. But without justice and equality, we would do little more than spin our wheels, tricked by an illusion of progress as conquest and acquisition. A culture built on the anticipation of next year's model was bound to run out of steam and was in fact in danger of being overcome by alienation, violence and sickness of spirit. That warning is the common ground shared by the prophecies of Du Bois and Martí.

Cornel West's reading of Emerson and Du Bois exposes the limitations of the American liberal tradition, the same tradition that Martí admired and questioned. In *The American Evasion of Philosophy: A Genealogy of Pragmatism*, Cornel West, quoting Santayana, writes that "Emerson is not a social revolutionary because he believes he is already on the right track and moving towards an excellent destiny" (17). Like Emerson, Martí cast himself in the role of prophetic seer, but unlike Emerson, he was a social revolutionary. According to West, Emerson's understanding of vision promotes "separateness over against solidarity, detachment over against association, and individual intuition over against collective action" (18). For Martí, without solidarity and collective action, individual vision was at best limited; at worst, Emerson's credo of enlightened individualism might be used to fuel an innocuous protest against American expansionism, or to justify torturing people on an assembly line. A nation as powerful and self-assured as the United States could afford the luxury of self-righteous protests against injustice. In fact, such protests, couched in the proper rhetoric, might even gain great cultural prominence. A spirit of protest might figure in a public debate or be implicit in prestigious works of art or literature. At the same time, protest can be either politically insignificant or unintentionally supportive of the very oppressions it seeks to counter. According to West, "Emerson's moral support for Indians and

Mexican sovereignty is well known, though his organic conception of history renders his 'against-the-grain' support rather impotent and innocuous" (34).

West suggests that an Emersonian tradition, which valued the individual over the herd, came to justify the subjugation of people who did not belong to the "Saxon race." For example, Emerson's faith in the potential of each individual was distorted in the macho pose of Theodore Roosevelt, whose contempt for "swarthy" Latins is well known. In his *Rough Riders* and other essays, Roosevelt writes that Cubans were incapable of fighting in a gentleman's war. They just got in the way of real men, the proud Spaniard and the heroic American, ready to take command from the defeated yet noble European. "To occupy my few spare moments," Roosevelt writes in a chapter titled "To Cuba" in *The Rough Riders*, "I was reading M. Demolins's 'Superiorité des Anglo-Saxons' [*sic*] (the superiority of the Anglo-Saxons)," a book he evidently admires, referring to its author as "the excellent French publicist" (47). In fact the title of the book by Edmond Demolins (1852–1907) is *A quoi tient la supériorité des Anglo-Saxons?* (What are the reasons for Anglo-Saxon superiority?). It is evident from his comments that Roosevelt was less interested in Demolins's answer than in providing his own. His "glorious" actions in Cuba were part of that answer.

Like Martí, Du Bois understood the chilling contradiction at the heart of American democracy: its ideals of equality and human dignity relentlessly undermined by an insidious racism. In an essay entitled "The Souls of White Folk," Du Bois writes: "Instead of standing as a great example of the success of democracy and the possibility of human brotherhood, America has taken her place as an awful example of its pitfalls and failures, so far as black and brown and yellow peoples are concerned" (*Writings* 937). In a letter to a friend, written from New York in November 1889, Martí says: "A man of color has the right to be treated according to his qualities, without any reference whatever to his color" (1:254).

Like Martí, Du Bois saw Emerson's vision of personal freedom degraded in various forms of vacuous self-promotion. In "The Sovereignty of Ethics," Emerson writes that "our institutions, our politics, and our trade, have fostered a self-reliance which is small, Lilliputian, full of fuss and bustle," devoid of reverence. Martí looked for ways to stay true to that reverence, guided by an expansive, committed version of Emersonian self-reliance. Like Du Bois, Martí professed his alliance "*con los pobres de la tierra*" (with the wretched of the earth). Like Du Bois, he believed in a "new appreciation of joy," in a "new desire to create," in a "new will to be" (Du Bois, *Writings* 995). Martí also had what Du Bois called his "island within," "a fair country" that would see him through every struggle and that allowed him to face death with stoic equanimity. For Martí the creations of others were his best teachers.

From Emerson's essay "Art," Martí learned that "the artist must employ the symbols in use in his day and nation to convey his enlarged sense to his fellow-men" (*Essays* 247). Martí lived in a constant struggle to communicate that "enlarged sense," knowing that, once others grasped it, freedom and creativity would fill their lives. Yet he also knew that prejudices of race, class, or social standing circumscribed the creative spirit, and that to smother this spirit in a single individual would do terrible damage to the whole.

Martí's method of appropriation itself is Emersonian. "The greatest genius is the most indebted man," Emerson writes in "Shakespeare; or, the Poet." The poet is "a heart in unison with his time and country" (*Collected Works* 4:109). In his essay on Emerson, Martí mourns the death of the man; at the same time, he rejects all mourning because the man he so admires came to embody his own nation. "Nation" in this case is not only the laws, traditions and prejudices of the republic but the place itself, its geography, its rivers and mountains. As a youth, the writer was a "young eagle," a "sapling," and as he grows, his proportions become gigantic. Martí compares Emerson's tall body to a tree, swaying in the pure air. His forehead becomes "a mountainside," and "his nose is like the beak of a bird that flies high over the mountains" (13:18). His voice is that of a "messenger of the future." Throughout the essay, Emerson most often appears as a mountain, a stony peak not softened by plants and flowers but jutting into the clouds. Ultimately, the writer becomes a heavenly body: "He radiated light as if from a star. He embodied the full dignity of humanity" (De él, como de un astro, surgía luz. En él fue enteramente digno el ser humano) (13:20). Martí constructs a dense web of metaphors and images, and the result is that a precise image of Emerson is lost. Even the name "Emerson" and the prejudices of the man are reduced in scope in the awesome landscape carved by Martí from fragments of the writer's words. In Martí's own web of words, the individual and the limitations of the human condition recede, and what remains is made of a harder, more lasting stuff, just and embracing.

Some of Martí's words no doubt echo the conventional praises published at the time of Emerson's death. At the same time, Martí goes beyond mere praise. He renders in Spanish something of the radical spirit that permeates the New Englander's words. Martí had to create new patterns for what he was doing. In his writing, he appropriated images from the Spanish mystics as much as he assimilated the radical modernity of Baudelaire. As a political activist he had to create new strategies to sustain coalitions and launch a war against a formidable enemy. There were no manuals, no theories that might guide any of his activities, so he created from whatever he could assimilate.

In Emerson Martí found not a system to follow but a light with which to create his own. Emerson, Martí writes, "obeyed no system, because to do so seemed like an act of blindness and servility; nor did he create one, for this he considered the act of a weak, base and envious mind" '(No obedeció a ningún sistema, lo que le parecía acto de ciego y de siervo; ni creó ninguno, lo que le parecía acto de mente flaca, baja y envidiosa)' (13:20). Martí realized that what Emerson meant by "Nature" was not the mere contemplation of a lush meadow or a pretty sunset. Nature in fact stood for a radical transformation of a human being's perception of the world and of the self. "He buried himself in Nature," Martí writes of Emerson, though now he could be writing of himself, "and emerged from her radiant, thus feeling like a man and therefore like a God."

In his readings of Emerson, Martí found what Bloom has called the "unsettling" of "the status of the self" (318). Bloom writes that "Emerson is no sentimentalist, and it is something of a puzzle how he ever got to be regarded as anything other than a rather frightening theoretician of life or of letters" (314). Emerson read "the Hindus," Martí writes, "who, tremulous and submissive, are present at the evaporation of their own soul" (13:21). Here "soul" is synonymous with "self," and the comment does not refer to its destruction but to its transformation. There is no "transfusion" without loss. There is no nihilism here; on the contrary, a transformed self is open to boundless possibilities, even in death. In the English version of Martí's "Emerson," included in *On Art and Literature*, "la evaporación de su propia alma" is rendered as "the evanescence of their own souls." In Esther Allen's translation, the literal rendering is more accurate, for it is an "evaporation" of the self, that is, its transformation not its annihilation (*Selected Writings* 120).

Martí grasped the seemingly chaotic aspect of some of Emerson's writings: "At times he appears to jump from one subject to another, and at first glance the relationship between two contiguous ideas is not readily apparent. The reason is that what to others is a leap, to him it is a natural step. He strides from mountaintop to mountaintop like a giant" ("A veces parece que salta de una cosa a otra, y no se halla a primera vista la relación entre dos ideas inmediatas. Y es que para él es paso natural lo que para otros es salto. Va de cumbre en cumbre, como gigante") (13:22).

Martí's gloss of Emerson would have tremendous impact on the development of Latin American literature. The Emersonian vision of the universe as a web of analogies, open to poetic appropriations, informs the work of the *modernista* writers who followed Martí, notably Rubén Darío (1867–1916). In *Nature*, Emerson writes that analogies "are constant, and pervade nature. These are not the dreams of a few poets, here and there, but man is an analogist, and studies relations in all objects" (*Collected Works* 1:19). This is the cornerstone of Martí's own work. Again echoing Emerson, he writes in "Dos patrias," "El universo/ habla mejor que el hombre" (The universe speaks better than man). In *Children of the Mire: Modern Poetry from Romanticism to the Avant-Garde*, Octavio Paz (1914–1998) quotes Martí's entire poem, explaining that it contains all the great Romantic themes. More importantly he adds, it is a phrase that is at the heart of all the poetry of its time. Paz writes that it is a "phrase that no other poet in our language could have written before him," a phrase, he goes on to say, that "contains everything that I have been trying to say about analogy: 'The universe/ speaks better than man'" (100–101).

Nobel laureate Octavio Paz understood that Martí did not set out to create a type of poetry that others might imitate. What attracted Martí to Emerson was certainly not a style or a trove of images he might translate and recycle among his Spanish-speaking readers. What he found was a new cosmology that might sustain his own radical project: transforming his own self in order to lay the foundations of a democratic republic. Martí did not show great enthusiasm for conventional religions, but he relied on God to lift his spirits in the modern city and to give him the strength to face war and to embrace death if necessary. He found an image of his own God in Emerson's belief that "everything created has something of the Creator in itself; that everything will eventually come in the end to the bosom of the Creative Spirit" (cada cosa creada tiene algo del Creador en sí, y todo irá a dar al cabo en el seno del Espíritu creador) (13:24). What follows is a breathless series of quotations, translations and paraphrases, culminating in the image of an avid reader:

And thus the eyes of the one who reads run through those radiant and serene pages, which seem to have been written thanks to a superhuman grace, on the top of a mountain, by a light that is not human: thus the eyes stare, burning with desire to see these seductive marvels, and to roam through a palace of truths, through this procession of glowing pages that look like mirrors of steel that reflect glorious images, on eyes angered by so much light.

Y así corren los ojos del que lee por entre esas páginas radiantes y sere-
nas, que parecen escritas, por sobre humano favor, en cima de montaña, a
luz no humana: así se fijan los ojos, encendidos en deseos de ver esas
seductoras maravillas, y pasear por el palacio de todas esas verdades,
por entre esas páginas que encadenan y relucen, y que parecen espejos
de aceros que reflejan, a ojos airados de tanta luz, imágenes gloriosas.
(13:24)

This is an intense version of "the pleasure of the text." But reading is not
only a refuge from the chaotic city; it is the creation of a new city as "the
palace of truth," a specular place that gives the reader a new vision of the
self, translated and "transfused." This is the pronominal uncertainty of
"I" or "you" taken to a transcendental level. In an article on Martí as
reader of Whitman, Doris Sommer refers to the specular reverie of a
Latin American subject, who through reading incorporates a foreign
text. "And after Latin Americans set the grammatical shifters in motion,"
Sommer writes, "how can one be sure who occupies which position?"
("José Martí, Author of Walt Whitman" 78).

Alluding to Emerson's "The Over-Soul," Martí writes that "the
human soul, in its journey through Nature, finds itself within all of
it; that the beauty of the Universe was created to inspire desire and ease
the pain of virtue, and to encourage man to seek and find himself" (que
el alma humana, al viajar por toda la naturaleza, se halla a sí misma
en toda ella; que la hermosura del Universo fue creada para inspirarse el
deseo, y consolarse los dolores de la virtud, y estimular al hombre a
buscarse y hallarse) (13:24). This is the glory missing at the art auctions
in New York, where the aim is to find precious objects to fill the gaps
in a spotty genealogy, or to cover the empty walls of a Fifth Avenue
mansion. In an 1887 article on New York galleries, Martí describes
rich New Yorkers at an auction of European paintings, where the auctioneer is transformed into a bird of prey, his voice pecking around
the room. The auctioneer jokes and panders to the crowd, for he
knows that "these rich New Yorkers would rather have the glory of
pretending to be descendants of a palace pimp or of the doorkeeper
of a monarch than the true glory of creating their own selves" (El
sabe que estos ricos neoyorquinos prefieren a la gloria verdadera de
crearse a sí propios la de parecer descendientes de algún buscamozas
o guardapuertas de monarca) (19:314). Martí's glory is in the recreation
of the self, a project that is open to the future and that is available
to all. It is synonymous with "freedom" and has nothing to do with
the relative value of one object or another, what the auctioneer
calls "art."

In Martí's reading of Emerson, "commerce with nature and the government of one self" must inform our every move. The individual is not placed in this world to impose his or her will but to learn to read a "universal order" in all things and to bring that wisdom to the creation of all human things. In his paraphrase of Emerson, Martí lays out a program for self-liberation that is also the only worthy base for a just society, founded on the "similarity between all living beings; the equal composition of all the elements of the Universe" (la semejanza de todos los seres vivos; la igualdad de la composición de todos los elementos del Universo) (13:25).

Martí comes to the realization that self-liberation is inseparable from self-sacrifice. Today the equivalence of the two may be difficult to grasp. From a contemporary perspective, liberation of the self is a private declaration of independence, a coming out of whatever closet it was trapped in. It is the opposite of self-sacrifice, which sounds like the sentimental, often half-hearted erasure of the self. For Martí the two options did not represent polar opposites, but rather two sides of the same coin, the only currency worthy of circulation in a true democracy.

In *Nature*, Emerson writes: "The ancient Greeks called the world *kosmos*, beauty" (*Collected Works* 1:12). The distant meaning of "kosmos" as "beauty" may be glimpsed in the lowly word "cosmetic," from *kosmein*, "to adorn or beautify." When Martí writes that the object of life is "the satisfaction of the yearning for perfect beauty," he does not mean the yearning for the perfect house, or the perfect body, or for a perfectly crafted sonnet for that matter. It is rather the desire to approach an understanding of the cosmos and our place in it, and to represent that desire with whatever talent and whatever tools we may possess. "The books of the Hindus" are one of the sources of such understanding. At the time Martí was writing, their influence was beginning to spread in Europe and the Americas. Martí called them "those resplendent books," though it is likely that his knowledge of them comes directly from Emerson's appropriation of the Hindu and Buddhist scriptures. In Martí's papers there is a brief note about "the generous, conciliatory, serene, just, tolerant, loving philosophy of Buddha" (21:260).

Through the wisdom of "Indian philosophy," Emerson learned "to look at Nature through the eyes of others because he has found those eyes to be like his own, and thus sees darkly and discredits his own visions" (a ver la naturaleza a través de ojos ajenos, porque ha hallado esos ojos conformes a los propios, y ve oscuramente y desluce sus propias visiones) (13:27). In this wisdom, the human creature is "sweetly annihilated." In a passage that might have been written by Borges, Martí considers what happens when an individual begins to understand this esoteric knowledge:

> And then he wonders if Nature is not a phantasmagoria and man a fantasizer, and the entire universe, an idea, and God the pure idea, and the human being the aspiring idea, which will in the end come to rest in the bosom of God, like a pearl in its shell or an arrow in a tree trunk. And he begins to build a scaffold and to construct the Universe. But immediately he brings down the scaffolding, ashamed of the baseness of his edifice and the poverty of his mind, which, when it insists on building worlds, looks like an ant, dragging a mountain chain behind its back.
>
> Y se pregunta entonces si no es fantasmagoría la naturaleza, y el hombre fantaseador, y todo el Universo una idea, y Dios la idea pura, y el ser humano la idea aspiradora, que irá a parar al cabo, como perla en su concha, y flecha en tronco de árbol, en el seno de Dios. Y empieza a andamiar, y a edificar el Universo. Pero al punto echa abajo los andamios, avergonzado de la ruindad de su edificio, y de la pobreza de la mente, que parece, cuando se da a construir mundos, hormiga que arrastra a su espalda una cadena de montañas. (13:27)

After a failed attempt the desire to build and create returns, but now instead of failure, there is renewal. In this ebb and flow of aspiration and descent, the human creature is guided by intuition, allowing the beautiful to stand and demolishing what is false. Having sat "in the senate of the stars and returned strong," you "may now sit in the senate of the people." The creations of poetry and literature are representations of beauty, *kosmos*, because they throw light upon the mystery of the universe. Without such light, "man" may conquer the world and yet remain prisoner of his fears or even of his own power. Poetry, as a force of nature embodied in a human being, whether a poet, a painter or a dancer, produces this light. It counters what is mean and base and can turn abjection into victory. Writer and political activist Audre Lorde (1934–92), born in New York City to parents from the Caribbean, gives a definition of poetry as light that, in one of Borges's improbable universes, might have been written by Martí: "Poetry is not a luxury. It is a vital necessity of our existence. It forms the quality of light within which we predicate our hopes and dreams toward survival and change, first made into language, then into idea, then into more tangible action" (37).

Among Martí's notes is an undated fragment that describes a longer version of "the evening of Emerson" (la tarde de Emerson), mentioned above, in which he describes the loss of self and its "transfusion" into the world. Martí probably wrote this longer version of "the evening of

Emerson" in his office on Front Street, on the top floor of a walk-up building with views of the city. The reference to "stars" in the passage, quoted below, suggests that it is late afternoon or early evening. *Tarde* in Spanish can mean both "afternoon" or "early evening." I have opted for the latter meaning. In the passage, the writer is no longer reading Emerson but thinking about him, and this thought generates a vision of the future. It presents a rare glimpse of Martí by himself, neither the orator nor the hero, but a writer alone in his study, stripped to the waist, perhaps reflecting on the day's work as he gazes at the city down below. The passage recalls the brief text "Borges and I," in which a series of disconnected preferences and whims defines a subject not just fragmented, which suggests the flatness of a puzzle, but composed of dynamic particles, capable of infinite combinations:

> I have walked through life enough, and I have tasted its many flavors. Well then, the greatest pleasure, the only absolutely pure pleasure that I have enjoyed up to now was that evening when from my room, half naked, I saw the sprawling city, and I saw something of the future, thinking of Emerson.
>
> The life of the stars. At least, the brightness of stars. That impression is similar to those that the joy of friendship has produced in me, always superior to those offered by love, [similar] to the emotion that has seized me when hearing the voice of some singer or in the contemplation of a painting. And caressing the heads of little children. And this is the entire substance of my life, after thirty years.
>
> Ya he andado bastante por la vida, y probado sus varios manjares. Pues el placer más grande, el único placer absolutamente puro que hasta hoy he gozado fue el de aquella tarde en que desde mi cuarto medio desnudo vi a la ciudad postrada, y entreví lo futuro pensando en Emerson.
>
> Vida de astros. Por lo menos, claridad de astros. A esa impresión se asemejan las que el goce de la amistad me ha producido en grado siempre superior a los que el amor me ha dado, y la emoción en que ha solido dejarme suspenso la voz de algún cantante o la contemplación de un cuadro. Y acariciar cabecitas de niño. Y éste es todo el jugo de mi vida, después de treinta años (22:323).

This is Martí's brief portrait of the artist. He says he was 30 years old when he wrote this fragment, in 1883, a year after he published the essay on Emerson. Reams of paper were yet to be filled, along with the founding of the Revolutionary Party and the invasion of Cuba, not the projects of an artist but of a revolutionary. Martí had 12 years to live. By his own admission, everything he had done was an apprenticeship for the final return to his "vineyard," the hills of eastern Cuba, always an imagined home for someone who has up to now only "walked through life."

It was a home that only became real when Martí walked on it for the first and last time. In Oriente, the artist and the revolutionary finally became one. The record of that final journey is in the *War Diaries*. In Cuba's "vineyard" of course there are no grapes, only the plantains of Martí's "bitter wine."

CHAPTER 6

MARTÍ FACES DEATH*

Martí's diary is the record of a modest invasion that unleashed a war, but it is much more than that. It is a pilgrimage of the soul, the last stance of a Caribbean visionary faced with the mystery of nature, the power of human kindness and the glimmer of transcendence before the certainty of death. The *Diaries* are one of those stories that, in Andrew Delbanco's words, "leads somewhere and thereby helps navigate through life to its inevitable terminus in death; [and therefore) it gives us hope" (*The Real American Dream* 1). The *Diaries* are in fact two diaries in one. The first part, "From Montecristi [in the Dominican Republic] to Cap-Haïtien," begins on February 14 and ends April 8, 1895. The second part, "From Cap-Haïtien to Dos Ríos," covers from April 9 to May 17, 1895.

In the original manuscript, the first part of Martí's *War Diaries,* written in Haiti and the Dominican Republic, consists of a disordered collection of loose sheets of paper. The second part, written in the mountains of eastern Cuba, though apparently numbered by Martí himself, is at times barely legible. Martí did not write in his diary every day; he caught up whenever he had time, reconstructing recent events. Consequently, the dating and the sequence of events are not always clear. In places, the diaries are literally a palimpsest. Martí wrote in pencil, then went back over his own writing in ink, making changes and creating at times parallel versions of a phrase and its variant. Despite the admirable effort of editors, notably Mayra Beatriz Martínez and Froilán

---

*All references to Martí's diaries are from *Diarios de campaña*. Ed. Mayra Beatriz Martínez and Froilán Escobar; they are given parenthetically by page number. Unless otherwise noted, all other references to Martí's works, given parenthetically by volume and page number, are to *Obras completas*. Unless otherwise noted, all translations are mine.

Escobar, Martí's *Diarios de campaña* (war diaries) never quite settle on the printed page. Something of the precarious circumstances of their composition remains, adding to their aura as a unique, foundational text, ever on the fringes of literature.

The two parts of Martí's *Diaries* have distinct editorial histories. Critics have noted that there is a shift in tone and style from the first part to the second. The reasons for the shift are in part tactical. While organizing the final stages of an expedition to Cuba in Haiti and in the Dominican Republic, Martí and his allies had to exercise extreme caution. The names of people who helped them had to be kept secret. Agents working for the Spanish government kept track of the insurrectionists' every move, and did everything in their power to prevent them from going forward. Once in Cuba, however, Martí, Gómez and their allies joined a military campaign in a remote area, the mountains and dense thickets of eastern Cuba. Survival, not fear of discovery, was the order of the day.

However, a tactical shift does not account for the differences between the two parts of the diary, which constitute a sort of Caribbean diptych. In Haiti and the Dominican Republic, Martí is still the observer, recording quaint phrases and colorful details of manner and dress. Once in Cuba, Martí seems to breathe life into the landscape and the people who inhabit it. The process is reciprocal: The landscape and the people who inhabit it are a source of energy and inspiration. The diary then becomes a narrative whose core is compassion and gratitude, compassion for the human condition and gratitude for small yet crucial favors: a place to rest, a swallow of wild honey to quench the thirst of an uphill climb.

Referring to Martí in the *Diaries,* Lezama Lima has written: "We see him as a fragment of a totality that escapes us" ("Lo vemos como fragmento de una totalidad que se nos escapa") (580). What Martí demands, Lezama argues, is our participation in the "totality of the image," that is, in the totality of a representation that transcends human limits, including the nation and the self. Rafael Rojas has written of Martí's "intimate experience of fragmentation." Martí's resistance to the book did not prevent him from outlining some 50 book projects in his notes or suggesting to others what sorts of books they might write. Yet like Rousseau, Rojas points out, Martí wanted to write "in the hearts of men." Like Mallarmé, he set out to write "transcendental books," books that might make sense of diverse fragments, mere signals of an "Invisible Totality" (Rojas 123). The *Diaries* are the most complete example of this "book" made up of fragments that barely coalesce into a whole, whose precarious center shifts with a constantly moving subject, *hombre ambulante* (traveling man) in the expression used by one of the characters Martí encounters along the way.

By the end of 1894, Martí had masterminded a plan for a full-scale invasion of Cuba. On the island there was a network of conspirators and collaborators, organized by Juan Gualberto Gómez (1854–1933), Martí's longtime friend and ally. Gómez, a distinguished journalist and political activist, was a Cuban of African descent, no relation to the Dominican general Máximo Gómez (1836–1905), the commander of the insurrectionist forces. According to the plan, three fast vessels, rented for the occasion and commandeered in the high seas, would transport men and supplies to three different points in Cuba. One of the ships would leave from Central America, carrying Antonio Maceo and his troops. The two other ships planned to sail from Fernandina Beach on the north coast of Florida. After the invasion of Cuba at three strategic points, local opposition to Spanish rule would be unleashed in every corner of the island. Martí abhorred violence and dreaded the possibility of a long war; however, he had come to terms with "the necessary war," a just, heroic effort to rid Cuba of Spanish rule. His ambitious plan for a triple invasion would insure that Cuba's second war of independence, unlike the first, would be swift and decisive.

In January 1895, days before the Cuban insurrectionists were to sail from Fernandina Beach, a traitor told one of the captains of the vessels that the boxes being loaded into his ship were filled with arms. The captain alerted U.S. authorities, which seized the vessels, further proof that the United States not only would not support Cuba's struggle for independence but would do everything in its power to prevent it, preferring to wait and deal directly with Spain for a larger reward, Cuba itself. Martí had raised over $60,000 dollars to carry out this failed plan, a good deal of it from small donations given by cigar workers from New York, Tampa and Key West. Devastated but undaunted, Martí regrouped, quickly organizing a second invasion. However, the plan for a surprise attack against Spanish power and a swift, decisive war in Cuba was finished (Toledo Sande 235).

Martí left New York City on January 30, 1895, two days after his forty-second birthday. A week later he arrived in Santo Domingo, where he met General Máximo Gómez, the old yet formidable veteran of Cuba's first war of independence, *la guerra grande,* our Great War, best known as the Ten Years' War (1868–1878). General Gómez was the man chosen by Martí to lead the war that would put an end to Spanish control of Cuba. War against the Spanish government was already raging in parts of the island, and Martí was ordered back to New York to raise funds and organize the opposition in exile. However, when a Dominican newspaper claimed that Martí and Gómez were already in Cuba, Martí decided it would be advantageous to stay with Gómez and indeed go on to Cuba.

Martí, Gómez and their allies sailed from Montecristi, in the Dominican Republic, to the island of Great Inagua, the southernmost of the Bahamas, on board the schooner *Brothers*. Again, a tip to the local authorities put an end to the plan to continue on to Cuba. With the help of the Haitian consul in Great Inagua, Martí persuaded Heinrich Löwe, the captain of the German freighter *Nordstrand*, to take him and his companions back to Cap-Haïtien, with renewed plans to sail to Cuba. Aware of the expeditioners' plans, the U.S. consul in Inagua asked the British authorities to send a war ship out of Nassau with orders to pursue the *Nordstrand* and apprehend the Cuban insurrectionists. However, the *Nordstrand* escaped and hastily sailed from Haiti on April 11. Late that evening, in a fearsome gale, Martí, Gómez and four other men landed in a remote beach in eastern Cuba. Their small boat, which had been hoisted aboard the freighter, barely made it to shore. The *Nordstrand* sailed on to Jamaica (Toledo Sande 237–45). There were six men, General Gómez wrote in his own diary, and "anyone would say they were six madmen" (275).

Once in Cuba, Martí marched through the hills, thick with tropical vegetation, lugging a rifle, some maps and a knapsack weighing some 50 pounds. He also carried a Colt revolver, a Winchester rifle and the indispensable machete, a tool, a weapon and the very symbol of insurrection. Martí spoke to groups of armed men ready to join the war, while urging others to do the same. He established links with local sympathizers, wrote letters to potential allies, drafted communiqués to New York newspapers and wrote in his diary. Later in the march, he helped to care for the wounded.

The diary's final entry, dated May 17, was written on the spot where two rivers, the Cauto and the Contramaestre, flow together, a place simply called Dos Ríos (two rivers). On May 19, as he charged the enemy on his horse, Martí was mortally wounded. A Cuban scout, working for the Spaniards, finished him off with his Remington rifle. There is sadness in this final journey of a poet and intellectual determined to prove his mettle in the field of battle. Yet the diary is not a sad book; on the contrary, it is full of hope and even joy. Many of its details may seem alien to us today, yet they are grounded in real experiences. In fact, the very strangeness of some details transforms them. These are not merely the odd names of places, plants and animals. They are tokens of a new reality, or perhaps a reality newly perceived. In Martí's dialogue with nature, the commonplace becomes the source of a new insight, a fresh revelation.

In the diary, the details of a war in the making contrast with descriptions of everyday life in the Caribbean backwoods. "Description" is too weak a word to categorize what Martí wrote in his final days in *la manigua*, Cuba's wilderness. The name of a tasty root roasted on an open fire, the color of a wild flower, the sayings of local people are details so finely observed, rendered so precisely and with such sympathy, that they vibrate with the breath of what is real. No plant is too small, no ingredient of a dish too insignificant, no animal too paltry, to escape Martí's avid eye in his paradoxical journey: westward to Oriente. "The *Diary* is full of eyes that sparkle, of gestures that reveal a fine, modest reverence, of strong, discreet courtesies" (Vitier, *Lo cubano* 275).

The diary begins on February 14, 1895, in Montecristi, founded in 1506, on the north coast of the Dominican Republic, near the Haitian border. Cap-Haïtien is a port city at the base of Haiti's northern peninsula, an arm of land that reaches west toward Cape Maisí, the eastern tip of Cuba, barely 60 miles away across the Windward Passage. It is evident in the many letters he wrote during this period that Martí suffered great anguish over the outcome of his lifelong efforts to establish a free republic in Cuba. Yet there is in the diary a lightness and a joy: lightness of being, perhaps, and the joy of observing things as if for the first, and last, time. There is a feeling in the diary that is difficult to name but that is different from anything else found in Martí's copious writings. The style of the diaries is far removed from the stilted grandiloquence of some of Martí's contemporaries and from the rich, ornate prose he often used. There are rich details, and sentences consisting of a single word. There is an effort to reproduce the precise name of a plant or an animal, or to render the exact phrasing of a local aphorism.

In the manuscript of the diaries, there are blank spaces for some names Martí hoped to fill in later, the name of a new ally, for example, or the local name for a certain plant. Starting in the 1970s, Cuban researcher Froilán Escobar recorded the oral testimonies of children who met Martí during his final journey. In one of these accounts, a 91-year-old man recalls that Martí "never tired of nature. He learned it as he went along" (no se cansaba de la naturaleza. La iba aprendiendo) (Escobar 74).

It is not the case, as it may at first appear, that the style of the diary is simpler than that of the essays, though in fact many sentences are so sharply trimmed that they become telegraphic in their preciseness. In the backwoods of the Caribbean, Martí had little use for rich allusions and learned references, staples of literary and, at that time, even journalistic writing. People, plants and animals spoke to him in a new language, which the writer put on the page quickly, without the labored grandeur of more refined prose. Martí did not write about what he had read or even about what he knew but about what he saw and what he learned along the way. For him the journey proved to be a new way of seeing, which in turn required a new way of writing.

In the aphorisms shared by the people he met, Martí found an autochthonous, living version of the "natural philosophy" he had so admired in the writings of Emerson (9:42). It is knowledge based on the study of the world, wisdom passed down from older folks to young ones in sharp, memorable phrases. In the towns and villages of Haiti and the Dominican Republic, the language Martí heard was full of these maxims, echoes of classical sententiae. Martí wrote that language there was *añeja*, not simply "old" but "vintage," like a good wine. For Martí, the language of common folk was not a mere tool, an appendage or an ornament, polished in this or that school, displayed like a new hat and discarded once it went out of fashion. It was a revelation of each individual's character and of his or her position in the world.

It would not be fair to say that Martí romanticized country folk and their quaint ways. That would suggest a parade of local types decked out in "native costumes" for the benefit of a stranger, or a boatload of tourists, as might be the case in our own time. In fact, the people of the Caribbean described by Martí are distinct individuals, proud of a hybrid culture that has made them resourceful, elegant and urbane even in the most remote areas. Martí drew brief word portraits of the people he met along the way, based on their manner of speaking, their dress, their work, and the things they made. There is no attempt to define a "Caribbean character," though one gradually emerges: shy and evasive at first, then kind, hospitable, sentimental and loyal.

In the *Diaries,* the people of the Caribbean have preserved traces of native knowledge, especially evident in the use of plants as food and medicine. Their expressions have deep roots in Spain or in France. Their gestures, manners and wisdom reveal their African sources. Plants and animals still bear the names the Tainos gave them. The diary is a gallery of human portraits, all distinct and original yet part of a rich cultural pattern. The stereotype is always seen in isolation, a cardboard cutout of reality. The types described in the diary are all connected to others and to the living world that surrounds them. They are distinct individuals, their humanity condensed in a gesture or a look, and in the brief stories they share with others. And yet they are what they are because of a web of connections to others and to the world around them.

For instance, listen to Arturo, Martí tells us, as if pointing to the young man standing in front of him. Arturo talks about "the little hens that I'm raising for my wife." Arturo is a "handsome young man, with long, nimble legs, bare feet, a machete always in hand, and a good knife at his belt; and in his restless face, the color of earth, the eyes are wholesome and anguished" (24). Arturo is newly married, and his wife went off "to have the baby with her people in Santiago." Arturo asks a simple, yet loaded, question of the visitor: "Why is it that if my wife has a child, they say that she gave birth, and when Jiménez's wife has hers, they say that 'it was delivered'?" (24). Arturo's wife gave birth, *parió*, which is said of women and also of animals. *Parir* is commonly said of women who give birth, but the verb suggests a certain harshness or earthiness, depending on the tone in which it is said. In any case, women of the middle and upper classes, such as Jiménez's wife, would never use it to refer to the act of birthing, preferring the euphemism *dar a luz*, literally, and quite prettily, "to bring [a newborn] into the light."

Arturo's pointed question remains unanswered, but the answer is clear. Without the benefit of an imported theory of class, Arturo has explained class differences by contrasting two expressions used to describe the birth of a child. Concrete examples suffice. "And so along the way," Martí writes, "you pick up phrases," and these phrases complement his gallery of Caribbean portraits, not just visual portraits but images that incorporate a way of life and a way of thinking.

In Santo Domingo, Martí meets Jesús Domínguez, "father of many daughters, one with green eyes, eyebrows in a fine arch, a commanding head" (44). Her dress, though a bit rumpled, is crimson percale; her shoes are dusty and worn, but she carries a silk umbrella and has a flower in her hair. Her sister, plump and vivacious, wears a rose in hers. No detail is insignificant. Their brothers, "magnificent lads, with honey-colored eyes and brawny chests, do not know how to read." The young woman's dress is not simply red cotton but "crimson percale." There is in this and other portraits something of the provocative freshness of youth and the confidence that comes from having "a good home."

Foreshadowing the use of indirect dialogue, so prevalent in twentieth-century fiction, Martí paraphrases the conversation of the young people's father, producing a compact catalog of country wisdom, almost Biblical in its resonance. Jesús Domínguez says that he had been rich, and then was so no more, and when fortune ebbed, he kept his head high, not letting anyone know of his ruin. He then asked the land for his lost gold, and the land gave it back to him, in the form of an abundant harvest. That was the wisdom of the proud Dominican farmer: "En la mesa hay pollo y frijoles, y arroz y viandas, y queso del Norte y chocolate" (On the table there are chicken and beans, and rice and vegetables, and cheese from the North [the United States] and chocolate) (48).

On March 2, in Fort Liberté, Haiti, Martí found lodgings with a man named Nephtalí and his family. Without asking who sent him, the man's family served the visitor a hearty lunch, and for the road, "Nephtalí gives me some good cheese, empanadas and sponge cake" (146). When Martí, a little worried about his meager funds, takes his host aside to ask how much he owes him, the man "grips both my arms and looks at me reproachfully: 'Comment, frère? On ne parle pas d'argent, avec un frère' " (How's that, brother? There's no talk of money between brothers). "Y me tuvo el estribo, y con sus amigos me siguió a pie, a ponerme en la calzada" (And he held my stirrup, and followed me on foot with his friends, to lead me to the main road) (148).

On Martí's journey from the Dominican Republic to Haiti and on to Cuba, only the help and support offered by men like Nephtalí and his kind daughter allowed the expedition to go on. The only thing that people had to offer was precisely what was needed most: food and shelter. In the *Diaries*, the hardships of the expedition and eventually the horror of death are leavened at every turn by human kindness, and not insignificantly by the human gift for turning whatever the earth has to offer into good things to eat. The *Diaries* offer a Caribbean banquet, a table spread with backcountry cooking, some familiar, some exotic, every dish singled out by the appreciative guest.

Laguna Salada was the name of General Gómez's prosperous hacienda in the Dominican Republic. It was surrounded by fields of corn, tobacco, plantain, sweet potatoes and oranges. There were flowers in the garden, and in one spot, encircled by lilies, there was a large, bare cross over a grave. Mercedes, a Dominican woman, and Albonó, a Haitian worker, served them white rice, chicken roasted on an open fire, sweet potatoes and *auyama,* a type of squash. They also served bread and cassava, which Martí preferred, and of course homegrown coffee, sweetened with honey.

In remote, isolated areas, Martí found order and cleanliness in the way that the families that welcomed him arranged their lives. Critics have mentioned the utopic qualities of the *Diaries,* especially suggested by an unwillingness to dwell on the treachery of others. However, Martí's Caribbean is no utopia; there is danger, poverty and isolation. On the other hand, what is meanness of spirit in others is deflected or nearly silenced, while the focus remains on the power of human dignity, even in less than ideal circumstances. In this sense, the *Diaries* are not merely the record of past events but the final testimony of one man's vision of a possible future. In Martí's version of the Caribbean, there is poverty, but not the abjection of helpless victims.

One of Martí's guides along the border between Haiti and the Dominican Republic was a local Dominican leader named General Corona. Martí tries to give a sense of the man's speech and quotes this homegrown definition of politics: "I don't know much about high politics, but to me right here in the way I feel, I think I know that politics is like a duty [imposed by] dignity" ("yo de aita política, no sé mucho, pero a mí acá en mi sentimiento me parece saber que política é como un debé de dinidá") (124).

Martí takes us through each home he visits, pointing out details that reveal how even a modest prosperity, wisely used, can create surroundings that comfort the body and feed the soul. One such house was Manuel Boitel's "casita," where everything showed evidence of an "industrious hand." Boitel farmed his own land; as a hobby he carved wooden toys: a diminutive cart to haul beams, a fancy carriage, painted yellow and black, tight and neatly turned. Indeed, in the mind's eye, Boitel's immaculate house appears as a self-contained world put together by a master craftsman. On the living room table, there were some old books, among them an old Protestant Bible and a treatise on apiculture. Martí and his hosts sat in chairs and rockers carved and decorated by Boitel. In the garden: sweet basil, bladder senna, cotton and spikenard. Martí picked some flowers for Rafaela, a neighbor's wife (70).

In Santiago de los Caballeros, on February 15, young people from the area gathered for a party honoring the guests, who are welcome with great fanfare. "The *charanga* (Caribbean band) receives me with a local waltz, light and guarded, to the tune of a piano and a flute, with guiro and tambourine" (Me recibe la charanga, con vals del país, fácil y como velado, a piano y flauta, con güiro y pandereta) (72). Martí writes about the lively conversation with his Dominican friends. Among other things, they talked about books and about the need for itinerant teachers. They discussed a book someone might like to write about local customs and legends. They chatted about architecture and the new houses in the city, full of light and air. Martí's lonely stance in the crowds at Coney Island offers a sharp contrast to these moments of tropical conviviality. Martí did not lack friends in the distant city, but the frenetic pace of his daily routine, along with the climate and ambiance of the metropolis, defined a radically different world. In the diaries, Martí records a different sort of human contact, marked by the subtle emotions that define the camaraderie and intimacy of good friendship, accompanied by lively music.

Taken as discrete units, truncated in an anthology for example, Martí's descriptions of the country are colorful vignettes, arranged for the benefit of a sensitive outsider. However, in the setting of the diary, the layering of details achieves a different effect. Like music, these scenes envelop the writer and his readers. Martí uses the first person with discretion if not with a certain reticence, but the reader knows that he was really there, and this "being there" manifests itself in the enduring power of the words we read today. On March 4, on the way back from Cap-Haïtien, Martí heard the music of "the Haitian sorcerers": "The body feels as if it were wrapped in a garment of music" (Como en ropa de música se siente envuelto el cuerpo) (186).

As we travel from one home to another, from *batey* to riverside, from a proudly served feast to a modest *cafecito*, something begins to change. We begin to see nature and the people that inhabit it in a different light, literally a new illumination, both real and symbolic. Reading the diary, I am reminded of these lines from Wordsworth's "Tintern Abbey": "For I have learned/ To look on nature, not as in the hour/ Of thoughtless youth; but hearing oftentimes/ The still, sad music of humanity" (207). Martí never had a "thoughtless youth," but he echoes Wordsworth's appreciation for the coming of the "philosophic mind," life's sweetest reward.

On February 14 at dawn, on the way from Santiago de los Caballeros, the old city founded in 1507, to La Vega, the "vague light" of the tropics speaks for itself, and "it was good for the soul, so soft and deep, that brightness," Martí writes. On either side of the road, there was "the nature of our America" in all its glory. The mango tree was full of flowers; the oranges, ripe. You could see mountains in the distance, and along the way, the country in full bloom, so beautiful that even the horses pranced more elegantly. On either side of the road, there were coconut trees, heavy with fruit, topped by their rough headdresses; there was the huge *ceiba*, our sacred tree, "whose strong arms open high in the sky," and the stately royal palm. Tobacco leaves burst from behind a fence, and the brook was trimmed with *caimitos y guanábanos*, star apple trees and soursops, their names paling in the translation. These sights fill our hearts with power and faith, Martí writes: "De autoridad y fe se va llenando el pecho" (78).

Evening in the tropics has become a promotional cliché, a cardboard cutout with palm trees and canned breezes: come to our island, the poster beckons. In the diaries, the tropical dusk is alive with sensations, not only what may be seen but also what is experienced with the entire body. The coming of night intensifies the spell cast by the landscape.

The traveler writes that he admired, "with the love of a son, the eloquent calm of the vibrant evening, and a group of palm trees, one leaning against the other, and the stars shining over their plumed crests" (80). In such as a setting, the senses open to allow for a kind of satori, Zen's sudden awareness, a time when everything achieves "a sudden, perfect cleanliness." It is "the revelation of the universal nature of man," Martí writes. It is a moment when the self fades, when it gingerly steps aside in order to yield its centrality and its fleeting authority to a greater good, present in the landscape and in the love of others, available to anyone with the wisdom to recognize it.

During another stop, Martí retreats to a corner, where a curious little boy follows him. "Yo, en un rincón" (I, in a corner [of the room]), Martí writes. He then draws an image for the boy, "on the back of a useless letter" (80). The "I" is in a corner, out of the way, and the letter is said to be "useless," as if the self and the authority of the written letter were set aside for the moment. The focus is on some clumsy figures on the walls, drawn by the boy with a red pencil. What is central is the contact with this boy, through a shared love of tracing images on paper.

The rhythm of the first part of the diary is defined by the transitions, now gentle, now abrupt, between reality and vision, between an insignificant detail and its transformation into a key to another level of perception. After a moment of vision, Martí simply records the proper feeding of a fighting cock, the pride of many a countryman. Beef, milk instead of water, and corn, thoroughly mashed. Manuelito, a local boy, "goes to move a yellow-striped rooster, which turns on him, its neck feathers bristling, ready for a fight. From the house they bring us coffee with anise and nutmeg" (82).

On March 3, or perhaps early the next morning, after staying with Nephtalí, the man who called him brother, Martí went to get a haircut, only to hear a lesson in identity politics, still provocative over a hundred years later. In a paragraph that might be inserted seamlessly in a story by García Márquez, Martí describes the barber and his shop. The barber is a small man, spiffy and sharp, and the barbershop is papered with old prints. Six paper roses dangle from the high ceiling. As the barber clips away, his new customer interviews him. The man's name is Martínez, and he says he "used to be from St. Thomas." Used to be? You mean you're no longer from St. Thomas, the visitor asks. No, now I am a Haitian, the man answers. And then offers this revealing conclusion: "I am the son of a Dane, not worth a thing; I am the son of an Englishman, not worth a thing; I am the son of Spaniard, even worse: Spain is the most wicked nation in the world. For a man of color, nothing is worth anything": *nada vale de nada* (180–82).

The barber who cut Martí's hair says he is a Haitian, even though he came from St. Thomas to earn a living. Survival, not national identity, is his thing. In the barber's world, nationalism is a meaningless abstraction, concocted by white men. Obviously intrigued by the man from St. Thomas, Martí insists, "So you don't want to be a Spaniard?" And the spiffy barber replies, "I don't want to be a Cuban, or a Puerto Rican or a Spaniard." The man concludes his harangue with a chilling prophecy about Puerto Rico. As a smart white Spaniard, he reasons, he might get five hundred a month for being governor of Puerto Rico, but as a native of Puerto Rico, never!: (Si era blanco español inteligente, sí, porque le doy la gobernación de Puerto Rico, con $500 mensuales: si era hijo de Puerto Rico, no) (182).

Martí closes this entry without a comment, letting the man's words speak for themselves. After the United States invaded Puerto Rico in 1898, all governors came from the United States until 1948, when Luis Muñoz Marín (1898–1980) took office. In Martí's record of a quest to found a new nation, the barber's words introduce what today we might call a subjective deconstruction of national identity. The barber spells out an unraveling at the heart of the very idea of national identity, which counters Martí's own life-long arguments in its favor.

For the Haitian barber, his origins are worthless, for they are the useless patrimony of white scoundrels. At the same time, his poor barbershop is also a kind of refuge for a ragged yet not unappealing aesthetic—six paper roses dangling from the shabby ceiling. The barber, unmarried because he is *hombre ambulante,* like Martí "a traveling man," has his say. In the stories of others, Martí's own voice finds a new echo, and through the writing of the diary, this echo figures in the making of a new nation, not the monolithic construct of flag-waving nation-builders but something more malleable and more enduring.

On March 25, 1895, in a letter written in Montecristi, three weeks after the visit to the barber, Martí again takes up the question of national identity in an impassioned plea for transnational Caribbean solidarity. In the letter, known as his political testament, Martí addresses his longtime friend Dominican writer Federico Henríquez y Carvajal (1848–1925) as *amigo y hermano* (friend and brother). Martí writes that "the free Antilles will save the independence of our America . . . and perhaps accelerate or determine the equilibrium of the world" (4:111). In a restatement of the ideas developed in "Our America" and other essays, Martí argues that this "equilibrium" cannot be achieved through an exclusive, aggressive nationalism but rather through cooperation across borders, or over the water, in the case of the Caribbean.

The difference in this final formulation of the politics of continental solidarity so dear to Martí is that he explicitly questions the limits of his own personal/national identity, a move that prefigures the contemporary cultural and political debates that have coalesced around the richly problematic notion of identity. For example, Gilroy distinguishes between identity as a "noun of process" (252), embracing and tolerant of others, and identity as "an indelible mark or code somehow written into the bodies of its carriers" (104). When identity is a process, rather than a label, "[i]ts openness provides a timely alternative to the clockwork solidarity based on outmoded notions of 'race' and disputed ideas of national belonging" (Gilroy 252). When identity is embattled, behind real or symbolic walls, otherness is a constant threat. Martí's lifelong struggle to create a Cuban nation, and to define a Cuban identity, was also a struggle against identity based on fear and exclusion.

After arguing that Caribbean unity is essential to continental autonomy, Martí asks his Dominican friend:

> Why should I speak to you about Santo Domingo? [the Dominican Republic]. Is that something different from Cuba? Are you not a Cuban, and is there anyone better at being one than you? And Gómez, is he not a Cuban? And I, what am I, and who can secure the ground [beneath my feet]?
>
> De Santo Domingo ¿por qué le he de hablar? ¿Es eso cosa distinta de Cuba? ¿Vd. no es cubano, y hay quien lo sea mejor que Vd.? ¿y Gómez, no es cubano? ¿Y yo, qué soy, y quién me fija suelo? (4:111)

Like the barber from St. Thomas, Martí suggests a fluid, contingent notion not only of identity but of subjectivity itself, a subjectivity dependent on love and solidarity with others not on the univocal, discrete affirmations of a tyrannical self. Even as he writes in his diaries about the joy of finally stepping on Cuban soil, to risk, in fact, to lose his life for the sake of the Cuban nation, Martí writes that the very ground beneath his feet cannot be easily fixed or secured. This is not the sort of contradiction that can easily yield to the spiritual or historical syntheses often associated with Martí's quest. The contradiction itself is the source of the energy that make Martí's life and work still resonant today. It should not be suppressed in order to allow the sacrificial Martí, ready to give up his life for his patria, be the only possible representation.

The Martí of the letter to Carvajal is not the triumphant Martí "dying with my face to the sun." It is a different man, a different "I": "And I, dragging my broken heart" (Y yo, a rastras, con mi corazón roto) (4:111). Separating the man from the myth is futile; both vie for space on the page, and both get it. Only the limitations of our own readings privilege one over the other.

On March 30, in Montecristi, Martí bought the schooner *Brothers* from a man named John Bastian, who promised to take the expedition to Cuba. The following day, Martí sailed from Montecristi, along with General Gómez, four crew members and four other allies: Francisco Borrero, Angel Guerra, César Salas, all three Cubans, and Marcos del Rosario, a Dominican. Before leaving, Martí wrote to Gonzalo de Quesada, his friend and literary executor. This last letter to Quesada is known today as Martí's literary testament. "Do not put those papers in order, nor make literature out of them . . ." he wrote. "Not a page I have written about Cuba seems to me worthy of her: only what we are about to do seems worthy." Despite this disclaimer, Martí's letter includes specific instructions regarding the publication of his poems and of his essays about the United States.

What Martí mistrusted was not writing but the modes of literary production that were dominant in his day. He was especially skeptical about the marketing of literary objects, bound tomes priced by the bookseller and lined like pretty hats in a shop window. Like any good writer, he knew that today's well-turned phrase might be fodder for parody in less than a generation. Martí never rejected words, but especially in this final journey, words had to resonate against real things and living people. In the Cuban countryside, Martí transformed Emerson's teachings into a subjective practice that allowed him to define, as stated in the opening of *Nature:* "an original relation to the universe"; "a poetry and philosophy of insight and not of tradition" (*Collected Works* 1:7). Martí's ambivalence toward literature was not a rejection but a radical rethinking of the individual's relationship to literary tradition, as critics such as Enrico Mario Santí, among others, have pointed out (*Escritura y tradición* 188).

At the same time, Martí needed a literary marketplace in order to survive. In a letter to his friend Manuel Mercado, he writes of the need to stay in New York precisely because of its central location and access to the "literary marketplace" or *mercado literario,* the term Martí uses. Ramos concludes that Martí in fact valued the emergence of a literary market, "separate from the institutions of the State" (Ramos 62). The absence of such separation had embroiled Martí in local political intrigues that had forced him to leave Guatemala and Mexico. For all its horrors, New York offered a neutral space, and a great location: *un lugar céntrico.*

A reader of the *Diaries* is frequently reminded that Martí's most pressing task was not writing but finding a boat that would take him and his friends-in-arms to Cuba. Two of the men from the *Brothers* schooner jumped ship. Bastian, the captain, proved to be untrustworthy. He claimed he could not find enough sailors for the journey when in fact he was persuading everyone he met to stay away from the expedition. After Martí managed to recover some of the money invested in the schooner, the expedition was postponed once again. Finally, as it has already been mentioned, Löwe, the captain of the *Nordstrand,* which was on its way from Mobile, Alabama to Jamaica, agreed to take the men from Inagua back to Cap-Haïtien then to a point near the Cuban coast, where they might make land in a small boat. As he waited to sail from Haiti, Martí turned his attention to the teeming world of the Caribbean port, ragged and ruinous, yet bustling and full of life.

It was while he waited that he wrote a vivid description of Palm Sunday at Cap-Haïtien, April 7, 1895. With his back to the door, Martí described the sounds he could hear outside, so that the reader's first impression of the busy port is aural rather than visual. Inside, he wrote at the captain's desk, in a place where there were books and mementos of a distant home. Outside, there is the sound of horses stumbling over the cobblestones, dislodged by the rain of the day before. There is someone saying "*le bon Dieu,*" and a cane tapping on the sidewalk, the sound of an open shoe, the Caribbean *chancleta,* dragging along. The writer hears the harangue of a local preacher, "in magnificent French," railing against "the merchants of savage divinities" in "this strong, black nation." He finally peeks through the blinds, and the reader along with him, to see the audience gathered around the preacher: "a drummer, two laughing boys, a young man in a pink tie, pearl-gray trousers, [holding] a cane with an ivory handle," a Haitian dandy in his Sunday best (224–28).

In the context of the diary, the incongruity of this scene is startling. Martí and his friends would soon be in Cuba, risking their lives in a war of independence, yet he writes about male fashions with the eye of a Parisian critic. In fact, the presence of the Haitian dandy in a war diary may be startling, but it is not incongruous. The diary is not merely the record of an expedition. It is also a sampler of everything Martí did and wrote, and he could write fashion criticism with the best of them. The scene of the dandy in Cap-Haïtien is also a way to signal a break with the past. Once in Cuba, there will no more book-lined cabins, no more pearl-gray trousers and ivory-tipped canes. There will be, however, a new relation between the writer and the world around him.

After looking outside and seeing the crowd, the boys, the dandy and a woman in her fifties, with a shawl and a hat, a book of hours and a parasol, Martí turns back to his writing table. This entry of April 7 is a compact masterpiece, a fragment that might have been torn from some future work of fiction, the book that Martí never wrote but of which he left a fine blueprint.

As the festive Palm Sunday unfolds outside, the writer remains in his "hidden room." On the eve of his departure for Cuba, Martí is literally hiding from the authorities, who might put an end to the expedition at any moment. At the same time, Martí takes advantage of his refuge to read and write. He gives a messenger two pesos to get some books from the "Haitian bookstore" nearby. The bookstore owner, "the black gentleman of Haiti," Martí calls him, sent the books ordered, along with the two pesos. It is the record of one last kindness from the island nations that had offered food and shelter, and now books; the island that, despite the writer's protests against literature, has kept him writing. The first part of the journey, from Montecristi to Cap-Haïtien, ends here, on April 8. Cuba lies to the west, some 60 miles across the Windward Passage.

From Cap-Haitien, the freighter carrying Martí, his comrades and their small boat sailed northwest, back to Great Inagua. The next day, having rounded the Cape of Maisí, they approached Cuba's southern coast. Martí might as well have been crossing into another dimension. As a child and as a very young man, he had lived in Havana, 600 miles west of Cuba's rugged Oriente. Just before his eighteenth birthday, in January 1871, Martí was deported to Spain for his activities against the colonial government. In the years that followed, his stays in Cuba were short and fraught with danger. He briefly returned to Cuba in 1877, and the following year he came back to Havana and stayed for about a year. In 1879 he was again deported to Spain, where he stayed for about two months, going first to Paris, then sailing back across the Atlantic to the United States. In 1880 he arrived in New York, where he would remain until his return to Cuba in 1895, the journey recorded in the diary.

Martí, so closely identified with Cuba, lived his adult life as an exile, *un desterrado,* someone without a country, literally "without earth," without a piece of land to stand on, as *ambulante* as the barber from St. Thomas. Now, having dedicated every waking moment of his life to the cause of his country's independence, he finally returns, not through cosmopolitan Havana but in a small boat, landing on a deserted beach during a severe squall, in complete darkness, as far from the capital as the island's geography allowed.

After years of struggle, after so many failures, Martí finally stood on Cuban soil. The men rowed furiously in the rain until at last "a red moon looked out from under a cloud." They made land on a rocky beach, far away from a village or even a single house. Martí was the last to leave the boat. Two sentences, as compact as our language allows, describe this moment: "Salto. Dicha grande" (I jump out. Great joy) (242). The date was April 11, 1895.

The mystery of that joy pervades the remainder of the diary. For Martí, *dicha grande* must have been an inexpressible sensation of well-being that persists in the human heart even as the certainties of the material world begin to crumble. In the first part of the diary, in Haiti and the Dominican Republic, nature surrounds the observer, but there is also a sense of distance. As he prepared to leave Haiti, Martí wrote and ordered books from the corner bookstore. Once in Cuba, this sense of isolation and protection, the privileges of the writer, banish forever. Exposed to the elements and to the encroaching horrors of war, the distance between the observer and all that surrounds him, the gap between subject and object, narrows. To find a comparable moment in the Spanish language, one would have to look back 400 years, at the writings of San Juan de la Cruz (1542–1591) and Santa Teresa de Jesús (1515–1581), Spanish mystics whom Martí admired.

Martí was no mystic, but many critics have identified the power of analogy at the heart of his "natural philosophy." Martí's analogical thinking is present in a constant search for the interconnectedness of universal phenomena, and for a way to express those often elusive connections through language. Julio Ramos has written of Martí's "profoundly divided subject," marked by the opposition between acts and their precarious representation (*Paradojas* 169). Cathy Jrade has written of a power in Martí derived from "a vision that resists the limitations of preset cognitive structures" (28). José Olivio Jiménez has written of "this intuition of a universal analogy" in Martí's poetry, situating him in "an incomplete list," which includes Swedenborg, Baudelaire and Emerson, along with powerful traces of Hindu and Buddhist thought (179–82). The demonic side of the analogical vision is irony, the mode for registering human frailty, doubt and *desengaño*, which for the baroque writers meant both "disillusionment" and the "realization of the truth." There is irony in the barber's sharp dismissal of identity, but its impact recedes in the second part of the diary, yielding to a restated faith in the intuition of universal analogy. "For a few, inexhaustible days, from his arrival in Playitas to his death in Dos Ríos, nature and spirit were fused in his gaze" (Vitier, *Temas* 118).

The goals of the expedition that took Martí, Gómez and the others to Cuba were clear and specific: (1) recruitment for the cause of independence, (2) contact with insurgent leaders, (3) development of a strategy to push the revolution from east to west, (4) organization of a provisional government. The verb *arengar* appears frequently in the diary. Its English relative "to harangue" does not do it justice. "To harangue" has a negative connotation, which is almost absent in Spanish. *Arengar* has a positive political connotation. It means to use passionate language to move people to action. Martí was an expert at it. At every stop, in front of a peasant's *bohío,* at the encampment by the river, at the crossroads, Martí talked to people and turned bystanders into allies, and allies into fighters. The twentieth century has made us weary of war, but for some of the men and women who listened to Martí, sacrificing everything—comfort, home, family, crops in the field, even life—became a fearless option. Martí loathed violence, but he believed that a war against tyranny was a just war. Still unconvinced, we might ask, "What is tyranny?" Martí would have had a ready answer: Tyranny is the trampling of the rights of people to live and work, to thrive and be happy.

Martí's presence in Cuba was essential from an ideological and a tactical point of view. As the force behind the exile organizations that made war with Spain possible, his command post had been in New York. Indeed, it seemed that he might return there once the war effort was well under way. The Spaniards certainly did not expect him to come to Cuba. Other capable military leaders, such as the Maceo brothers, were already running circles around the enemy in Oriente. It made sense not to expose Martí, the mind and soul of the entire operation, to the dangers of the battlefield. On the other hand, once Martí landed in Cuba, word quickly spread, and the fires set during the previous war, the Ten Years' War, smothered by a shameful compromise with Spain, were rekindled. The war effort was no longer centered in the relative safety of exile. It was now in Cuba, and the isolated battles already raging in the countryside would be linked in a devastating pattern that would soon reach Havana.

Moreover, if Martí could prove his mettle in battle, he would inspire hundreds more to join in. He might then retreat in glory, leaving the fighting to others in order to conduct the affairs of the new republic. When some of the soldiers began to address Martí as *presidente,* he tactfully refused the title. General Gómez overheard the use of the honorific title and objected even more strongly. Martí was now a general, Gómez argued; besides, he was a delegate to the assembly of the revolutionary government, not its president. There was an embarrassing silence, Martí writes. If Martí's presence was necessary to spark the war that would sweep over the island, the nature of his future role in the new republic was not entirely clear. It is evident that the specter of this uncertainty weighed heavily on him. He found solace and a kind of liberation in nature, the sky, the rivers, the many plants and animals, the land and the people who passed through it.

In the first part of the diary, in Haiti and the Dominican Republic, the presence of death is suggested in a cross, a powerful reminder of mortality. There was also a cross surrounded by lilies on a grave in General Gómez's prosperous hacienda. At one crossroad, there was a wooden Christ under a metal canopy, "a French Christ, pink and delicate, on a green cross" (158–60). A month later, on April 3, the cross again appears in a majestic image taken from nature but recast with great effect. High up in the sky, like a flock of large crosses, black-winged flamingoes fly in perfect formation. Such grand symbols, even the symbol of the cross, would no longer serve on Cuban soil, where symbols of death are replaced by the real thing.

Once in Cuba, a brutal killing, the first in the diary, thrusts us into a different world, a place at once open to the four winds and tied to solid earth. Up on a tree, a soldier spied "the first *jutía*," a small rodent not unlike the North American opossum, though darker and usually plumper. Marcos the Dominican climbed the tree and cut the *jutía*'s head off with one blow of his machete. Skinned, salted and soaked in the juice of sour oranges, the animal was barbecued over an open fire. A pig carried off the orange rinds and the bloody pelt. This is one of many scenes in the life of an army on the move. Yet the killing of the *jutía* also signals the passage into the Cuban countryside. The *jutía*, a modest creature, has an almost totemic presence in the culture of rural Cuba. There are no ferocious beasts in the forests. The tiniest hummingbird and the smallest frog are native to Cuba. There are no threatening wild animals and no poisonous snakes. The flesh of the native *jutía* is dark and gamy, and no doubt tasty, especially salted, soaked in sour oranges and slowly roasted. Yet the suddenness of this killing is unsettling. Martí uses the verb *degollar*, a word that almost smells of blood and that means "to behead" or to slice the throat from ear to ear. There is something repellent about a pig carrying off the animal's flayed skin. In the second part of the diary, we are far from the almost picturesque scenes of the first.

In the Cuban part of the diary, Martí and his allies are at the mercy of the elements. The tourist industry has produced a tropics of eternal spring, where the visitor is caressed by balmy breezes in a perfect crescent of white sand. Missing from the postcard image are the searing noonday sun and the fury of sudden tropical squalls, harbingers of the devastation of hurricanes, from the Taino word *hurakan*. Far from towns and village, in the second part of Martí's diary there is constant exposure to the elements, which can offer the revelation of a quite evening but can also exhaust and destroy. Given a chance, people from the Caribbean look for shelter in a darkly shuttered room, away from the sun, or in the wide *portales,* the columned arcades that protect folks from sun and rain. The killing of the *jutía* brings the harshness of the Cuban outdoors into focus. "Outdoors" is the wrong word for our untranslatable *intemperie,* which is the severity of the weather (*el tiempo*), a learned word that is nevertheless commonly used, especially in the expression *a la intemperie:* exposed to the open sky, always somewhat threatening. This *intemperie,* like the chill of the Cuban morning, permeates the second part of the diary, enveloping Martí and all those around him. "We feel that nothing can shelter them, that no shield (whether Catholicism, nationalism or a simple regionalism) can protect them. Only the mystery of human warmth gives them a little shade" (Vitier, *Lo cubano* 274).

The marching army got its food along the way, killing stray cows and pigs, or taking whatever the land had to offer, coconuts, plantain, sugar cane, honey, wild coffee. On April 16, soldiers and people from the area arrived at the camp, sometimes bearing gifts of food: "Everyone with an offering: sweet potatoes, sausage, rose apple liqueur, plantain broth" (Cada cual con su ofrenda: buniato, salchichón, licor de rosa, caldo de plátano) (248). Food becomes central in a daily ritual of offering and acceptance. Yet at every turn along the path, newly carved from the thicket with machetes, violence and death lurk.

A month later, on May 10, the killing of a heifer is vividly rendered. General Gómez grabbed a machete from one of his bodyguards and opened "a red gash in the heifer's thigh." With another blow to its front legs, the animal fell to its knees. Another soldier clumsily stabbed it with his machete, once, twice, finally reaching the heart. The animal stumbled forward, then fell dead, a jet of blood spurting from its mouth. The men dragged it away. The killing of men and women would soon follow. Only nature is immune to the suffering of human beings, and Martí turns to it as if seeking a temporary refuge from the horrors of war. In nature, he begins to hear a new language. He is awed that, once attuned to it, he can understand something of its rumors: "The beautiful evening will not let you sleep" (La noche bella no deja dormir) (252).

In the tropics, the coming of evening is sudden and punctual. For a moment, dusk is not the loss of light but the coming of a different type of illumination. Vegetation is outlined in deep shadows, and the sounds made by insects and small animals produce a strange harmony. Crickets "whistle," but the sound made by a choir of lizards requires the coining of an onomatopoetic word: *quiquiquea*. In a moment such as this, the laws that govern the universe seem to be altered, and there is a new perception of sights and sounds, defining a world that floats at once within and outside the realm of everyday realities: "Through the shrill sounds, I hear the music of the woods [*la música de la selva*], soft and complex, as if made by the most delicate violins; the music wavers, entwines and unravels, opens its wings and alights, flutters and rises, always subtle and faint, an infinite, flowing melody. What wings graze the leaves? What diminutive violin, indeed, what waves of violins extract the melody, and the soul, from the leaves? What dance is this, the souls of leaves?" (252).

Martí's musical reverie ends abruptly, to return to the place where the army has camped: "We forgot about dinner; we ate sausage and chocolate and a slice of roasted malanga root. Our clothes dried by the fire." What is sublime in nature is glimpsed in passing, but a marching army has to move on, and the writer returns to the dutiful prose of a military diary. Writing has become a refuge and a way to participate, though haltingly, in a harmonious, soothing song. With the portals of perception thus attuned, beauty is everywhere, in nature, in plants and animals, in men and women, in their bodies and in the parts of their souls that they reveal in their stories.

Ramón and Magdaleno, the sons of a man who joined the rebels, have come to the front with their father. Before they go back home, on April 22, Martí captures them in a brief portrait: "Ramón, Eufemio's son, with his soft chocolate colored skin, like reddish bronze, his fine, perfect head, and agile young body. Magdaleno, with his magnificent shape, firm-footed, slim ankles, shapely calves, long thighs, full torso, graceful arms, and on a slender neck, his pure head, with its downy upper lip and curly beard, a machete in his belt and his straw hat, wide-brimmed and pointed" (260). Taken together, the two brief portraits, evocative of Whitman's delight in male beauty, are the very image of a young *guajiro* turned *mambí*, a Cuban country boy who one day will become a fighting rebel, a *mambí*.

The rules of war have always been ruthless against those caught raping and pillaging in the wake of a marching army. After a brief trial, some soldiers were condemned to death and executed on the spot. On one occasion, Martí interceded on behalf of two men, and their lives were spared. Others were not so lucky. Martí wrote that one man died bravely. He never lowered his eyes nor did fear show in his body. The man politely asked General Gómez if he should face the firing squad or turn his back. "Facing," the General replied, "*de frente*," and gave the order to fire. As a brief epitaph for the condemned man, Martí adds, "He was

brave in battle" (290). Another condemned man collapsed on the
ground, recoiling in horror.

In the first part of the diary, nature and death inhabit parallel universes. In the second, the music of nature and the agony of death are set
in counterpoint. As the diary comes to an end, the two lines seem to
converge. Martí stands at the point of convergence, witnessing to the
transcendence of nature and to the certainty of death. There is a perva-
sive sadness in his stance, but there is also stoic resignation tinged with
joy. It is either joy or an elusive emotion akin to it, sustained by the
knowledge of having done the right thing and of having learned something about the order of the universe, privileged knowledge not often
granted to ordinary mortals.

In one of his best known poems, Martí prophesized his own death
in nature, "facing the sun." The diary is the fulfillment of that
prophecy, a visionary's last stance, written during a grueling military
march and taken to the very brink of death. Martí's visionary quest,
however, is balanced in a fearful equilibrium with the realities of war.
The tactical, political significance of Martí's presence in Cuba has
already been mentioned. The Spanish authorities knew that with Martí
in Cuba, there would no turning back, no deals struck that might put
off the war for a few more years. That much was clear. What remained
unclear was the nature of the role that Martí would play in the new
republic.

Soon after their arrival in Cuba, Gómez had promoted Martí to the
rank of major general. No one doubted that Martí embodied the very
spirit of the struggle for independence, but Gómez wanted to establish
Martí's credentials in the military campaign and thus lay to rest long-
standing, pernicious attacks on Martí's credibility and on his qualities
as a leader. Many people believed that Martí would be the logical
choice for the presidency of the new republic. However, Gómez explicitly objected, feeling perhaps that such talk was premature and might
provide fuel for those who had unjustly attacked Martí as a self-serving
intellectual, not entirely trustworthy and interested in his own
advancement. For his part, Antonio Maceo, the other key figure in the
war, had expressed his admiration and even love for Martí. However,
Maceo had reason to fear that a civilian government might be forced
to make a pact with the enemy, and that Cuba would end up as an
autonomous province of Spain, or worse, as a colony of the United
States.

At end of the Ten Years' War, in 1878, Maceo had refused the terms
of surrender to Spain and had continued fighting on his own, finally
acknowledging defeat but setting the pattern for continued resistance

against the enemy. He would have no part in anything that might lead
to the repetition of such an outcome. He feared that Martí's insistence
on a democratic republic would be interpreted as a sign of weakness
and proposed instead the formation of a military junta, immune to any
plans that would compromise absolute, unconditional independence.
In fact, Martí agreed, but his insistence on a democratic government
troubled Maceo, who revealed his mistrust of Martí with characteristic
bluntness.

Martí's meeting with Maceo, recorded in the diary, took place on May
5, at the main house of a sugar plantation called La Mejorana. Maceo
had a reputation for elegant dress and an aristocratic bearing, and he
lived up to it on that day. "All of a sudden, some horsemen," Martí
writes. Maceo, wearing a suit of fine gray linen, rode in on a golden
horse, its splendid saddle studded with silver stars. The workers at the
sugar mill received the soldiers with jubilant cries. There was a festive
atmosphere, with food for one hundred people. They served "pure
rum" and green *aguardiente,* potent, homegrown liquor. Maceo and
Gómez whispered to each other. Then they asked Martí to come over,
to tell him that "Maceo has other ideas about government" (292). The
three men moved to an adjacent room to continue their discussion on
the future of Cuba.

Maceo's reluctance to agree to Martí's plan for a democratic government may be better understood in light of earlier events. The arms ship-
ment of the earlier expedition, out of Fernandina Beach, had been
confiscated by the United States, which would not tolerate an armed
invasion against Spain secretly launched from its shores. The loss of the
weapons was a terrible blow both to the finances of the Cuban cause and
to the morale of Martí and other organizers. Subsequently, Maceo
requested funds for his own expedition from Costa Rica, where he had
lived for some years. Strapped for money, Martí was forced to send a sum
that Maceo considered insufficient. When Maceo refused the terms of
the offer, Gómez and Martí went on with their plans but forced Maceo
to answer to General Flor Crombet, who had had a long running feud
with Maceo. Maceo was deeply wounded, but he relented and accepted
these conditions. However, at their meeting in La Mejorana, he bluntly
told Martí, "I love you less than I used to love you," referring no doubt
to the earlier reduction of his command.

There is more to the disagreement between Martí and Maceo. The
deep divide between country and city, between action and words,
between intellect and power, seems to engulf them. There was mutual
admiration and love between the two men. Martí wanted nothing more
than to secure Maceo's alliance, and Maceo would fight to his death for

independence. Yet, sadly, there were forces at work destined to separate the two men. Martí wrote bitterly that there was an attempt to "brand me as the citified defender of hostile impediments to the military movement" (294). Martí held his ground, and the meeting ended in an impasse, though Maceo's final words were loaded with implications. "You go that way," he said as he turned his horse in the direction of his troops, camped nearby.

Martí noted that Maceo had not invited him and Gómez to review his troops, a military courtesy extended to allies but forgotten by Maceo in his haste to leave. "Night is falling on Cuba," Maceo said, "and I have to ride for six hours." Night was indeed falling in more ways than one. Neither Maceo's nor Martí's plan would be carried out. Martí had less than two weeks to live. A year and a half later, on December 7, 1896, Maceo was killed in battle, along with Panchito Gómez Toro, General Gómez's son. Maceo and his troops were close to their goal of taking Havana, thus ending the war and achieving independence.

In the final pages of the diary, Martí marveled at the way that war can make us immune to horror. "How is it that the spot of blood that I saw on the road does not cause me to feel horror?" "Nor the half-dried blood on a head that now lies buried in the satchel placed there by one of our cavalrymen?" (270). How is it, one might add, that nature, so beautiful and soothing, can frame such horror with absolute indifference? Martí must face the horrors of a war that he started, not so much to keep horror at bay but to transcend it. In Martí's paradoxical vision, the certainty of death brings no despair but is tempered by a wisdom inscribed in the most insignificant things, freely offered by nature.

The last entry in the diary is dated May 17, two days before Martí's death. On the 18, he wrote a letter to his Mexican friend Manuel Mercado. Along with a note to General Gómez, written the following day, they were the last things Martí ever wrote. In the letter to Mercado, one of the most famous in Martí's voluminous correspondence, he expresses his fears about Cuba's future. Martí wrote Mercado about what he had learned from Eugene Bryson, a reporter from the *New York Herald* who had interviewed him two weeks earlier. Bryson had told Martí that the Spanish commander, whom he had also interviewed, assured him that "Spain would rather deal with the United States than turn the Island over to the Cubans." And there were people in positions of power in the United States who were eager for such a deal. There were also many Cubans, on the island and in the United States, fearful of independence and looking to the United States for a solution to

Cuba's problems. There are men in positions of leadership, Martí wrote, "content to have a master, whether Yankee or Spaniard, who would maintain their positions of leadership or create new ones for them as a reward for their roles as shameless mediators," that is, as paid gofers between Spain and the United States. These people, Martí, went on, are "disdainful of the powerful masses, this country's skillful and inspiring mestizo masses, the intelligent, creative masses of whites and blacks" (4:168). Martí's final words were as unequivocal as they were prophetic. If these "disdainful" people (*desdeñosos*) took control of Cuba, hateful divisions based on race and class would destroy all hopes for a democratic, independent nation.

It is true that Martí replayed the role of the prophet crying in the wilderness. Those he described in his last letter, who were disdainful of anyone who was not similarly privileged, yet unwilling to share privileges with others, in fact achieved prominence after the war. Still, Martí found comfort in human kindness and in the desire to remedy injustice wherever it might be found. "In the benevolence of other souls," he wrote Mercado, "I feel the roots of this love of mine, *este cariño mío*, for the suffering of mankind and for the justice that might remedy it" (4:169). In Buddhist thought, an understanding of karma, of the interconnectedness of all phenomena, leads to compassion for all living beings. At the end of the journey, Martí came to a similar understanding. The roots of his compassion for human suffering are grounded in the goodness of others: those who offer food, who provide shelter, who share their stories.

On the eve of his death, Martí seemed to possess absolute lucidity about everything: his sacrifices for the cause of Cuba, his misgivings about its future and his unshakable faith in love. "I know how to disappear," he wrote, "But my ideas [*mi pensamiento*] would not disappear, nor would obscurity make me bitter." A Spaniard by the name of Valentín had joined the insurrectionist troops, one of many who after years of living in Cuba had become disgusted with Spanish rule and had chosen to join the struggle for independence. As Gómez's assistant and cook for the troops, Valentín, and others like him, played a modest but important role. On May 17, in Dos Ríos, by the turbulent waters of the cresting rivers, Valentín helped to prepare a tasty meal for newly arrived soldiers, *alzados* recruited along the way: baked plantains and *tasajo*, jerked beef. In a final gesture, Valentín, the man Martí called *el español*, the Spaniard, brought him something to drink, fig leaves steeped in hot water, sweetened with honey. The diary ends with this simple offering from an enemy turned brother.

Two days later, Martí lay mortally wounded in the battlefield. An enemy soldier finished him off, and the Spaniards carried away the body.

A few days later, Martí was buried in Santiago de Cuba. His death has often been called a sacrifice, not just for the cause of Cuba but a sacrifice in the name of freedom and justice. However, Martí's greatest gift was not in his death, horrible as all others described in his diary. A greater gift is the enduring record of Valentín's final offering: something hot to drink, sweetened with honey.

Bibliography

I. Works Cited

Abel, Christopher, and Torrents, Nissa, eds. *José Martí. Revolutionary Democrat.* Durham, NC: Duke University Press, 1986.

Aguilar, Luis E. *Cuba 1933: Prologue to Revolution.* New York: W.W. Norton, 1974.

Ayers, Edward L. *Vengeance and Justice: Crime and Punishment in the 19th Century South.* New York: Oxford University Press, 1984.

Ballón, José. *Autonomía cultural americana: Emerson y Martí.* Madrid: Editorial Pliegos, 1986.

Bederman, Gail. *Manliness and Civilization: A Cultural History of Gender and Race in the United States, 1880–1917.* Chicago: University of Chicago Press, 1995.

Bejel, Emilio. *Gay Cuban Nation.* Chicago: University of Chicago Press, 2001.

Belnap, Jeffrey and Raúl Fernández, eds. *José Martí's "Our America": From National to Hemispheric Cultural Studies.* Durham, NC: Duke University Press, 1998.

Blight, David W. *Race and Reunion: The Civil War in American Memory.* Cambridge, MA: The Belknap Press, 2001.

Bloom, Harold. *The Poetics of Influence. New and Selected Criticism.* Edited with an introduction by John Hollander. New Haven, CT: Henry R. Schwab, 1988.

Burrows Edwin G. and Wallace, Mike. *Gotham: A History of New York City to 1898.* New York: Oxford University Press, 1999.

Cañas, Dionisio. *El poeta y la ciudad: Nueva York y los escritores hispanos.* Madrid: Cátedra, 1994.

Cott, Nancy F. *The Grounding of Modern Feminism.* New Haven, CT: Yale University Press, 1987.

Darío, Rubén. *Obras completas.* 5 vols. Madrid: Afrodisio Aguado, 1950.

De la Fuente, Alejandro. *A Nation for All: Race, Inequality and Politics in Twentieth-Century Cuba.* Chapel Hill: The University of North Carolina Press, 2001.

Delbanco, Andrew. *The Real American Dream: A Meditation on Hope.* Cambridge, MA: Harvard University Press, 1999.

——. *Required Reading. Why Our American Classics Matter.* New York: The Noonday Press, 1997.

Demolins, Edmond. *A quoi tient la supériorité des Anglo-Saxons?* Paris: Librairie de Paris, Frimin-Didot, (between 1897 and 1901).

Díaz Quiñones, Arcadio. "La guerra desde las nubes." *Revista del Centro de Investigaciones Históricas de Puerto Rico* 9 (1997): 201–227.

Douglass, Frederick. *The Life and Times of Frederick Douglass.* Hartford, CT: Park Publishing Co., 1881.

Dray, Philip. *At the Hands of Persons Unknown: The Lynching of Black America.* New York: Random House, 2002.

Du Bois, W. E. B. *The Souls of Black Folk*. 1903; New York: Dover Publications, 1994.

———. *Writings*. New York: The Library of America, 1986.

Emerson, Ralph Waldo. *The Collected Works of Ralph Waldo Emerson*. Introduction and notes by Robert E. Spiller. 5 vols. Cambridge, MA: Belknap Press, 1975.

———. *Essays*. New York: Harper & Row, 1951.

———. "The Sovereignty of Ethics." *North American Review* 10.12. (May 1878). Available at http://www.emersoncentral.com /sovereignty_of_ethics. htm.

Escobar, Froilán. *Martí a flor de labios*. Prólogo de Cintio Vitier. La Habana: Editora Política, 1991.

Estrade, Paul. *Los fundamentos de la democracia en Latino-América*. Madrid: Doce Calles, 2000.

Ette, Ottmar. " 'I Carry a Wound across my Chest': The Body in Martí's Poetry." In *Re-reading Martí*. Ed. J. Rodríguez-Luis. 35–52.

———. *José Martí: Apóstol, poeta, revolucionario: una historia de su recepción*. Trans. Luis Carlos Henao de Brigard. Mexico: Universidad Nacional Autónoma de México, 1995.

Ferlinghetti, Lawrence. *A Coney Island of the Mind*. New York: New Directions Books, 1958.

Fernández Robaina, Tomás. *El negro en Cuba 1902–1958: Apuntes para la historia de la lucha contra la discriminación racial*. Havana: Editorial de Ciencias Sociales, 1990.

Ferrer, Ada. *Insurgent Cuba. Race, Nation, and Revolution, 1868–1898*. Chapel Hill, NC: The University of North Carolina Press, 1999.

Foner, Eric. *The Story of American Freedom*. New York and London: W. W. Norton, 1998.

Foner, Philip S. *Antonio Maceo: The "Bronze Titan" of Cuba's Struggle for Independence*. New York and London: Monthly Review Press, 1977.

Fountain, Anne. *José Martí and U.S. Writers*. Foreword by Roberto Fernández Retamar. Gainesville, FL: University Presses of Florida, 2003.

Gilroy, Paul. *Against Race: Imagining Political Culture beyond the Color Line*. Cambridge, MA: The Belknap Press of Harvard University Press, 2000.

Gómez, Máximo. *Diario de campaña 1868–1899*. La Habana: Instituto del Libro, 1968.

Gónzalez, Manuel Pedro. *José Martí: Epic Chronicler of the United States in the Eighties*. Chapel Hill: University of North Carolina Press, 1953.

González-Echevarría, Roberto. "Martí y su 'Amor de ciudad grande': notas hacia la poética de *Versos libres*." *Nuevos asedios al modernismo*. Ed. Ivan A. Schulman. Madrid: Taurus, 1987.

González Veranés, Pedro N. *La personalidad de Rafael Serra y sus relaciones con Martí*. (Lecture at the Cultural Institute "Club Atenas," Cuba). December 17, 1942. Pamphlet.

Helg, Aline. *Our Rightful Share: The Afro-Cuban Struggle for Equality 1886–1912.* Chapel Hill: University of North Carolina Press, 1995.

Hewitt, Nancy A. "Engendering Independence: *Las Patriotas* of Tampa and The Social Vision of José Martí." *José Martí in the United States. The Florida Experience.* Ed. Louis A. Pérez. Tempe, AZ: ASU Center for Latin American Studies, 1995. 23–32.

Historia de Cuba. Havana: Editorial de Ciencias Sociales, 1981.

Horsman, Reginald. *Race and Manifest Destiny. The Origins of American Racial Anglo-Saxonism.* Cambridge, MA: Harvard University Press, 1981.

Jiménez, José Olivio. *La raíz y el ala. Aproximaciones críticas a la obra literaria de José Martí.* Valencia: Pre-Textos, 1993.

Jiménez, Onilda A. *La mujer en Martí. En su pensamiento, obra y vida.* Miami: Ediciones Universal, 1999.

Johnson, John. *Latin America in Caricature.* Austin, TX: University of Texas Press, 1980.

Jrade, Cathy. *Modernismo*, Modernity and the Development of Spanish American Literature. Austin, TX: University of Texas Press, 1998.

Kasson, John. *Amusing the Million. Coney Island at the Turn of the Century.* New York: Hill & Wang, 1978.

Kaye, Jacqueline. "Martí in the United States: The flight from disorder." In Abel and Torrents, eds. 65–82.

Kirk, John M. *José Martí: Mentor of the Cuban Nation.* Tampa: University Presses of Florida, 1983.

Lezama Lima, José. *Obras completas.* Mexico: Aguilar, 1977.

Lorde, Audre. *Zami. Sister Outsider. Undersong.* New York: Quality Paperback Book Club, 1993.

Lugo-Ortiz, Agnes I. *Identidades Imaginadas: Biografía y nacionalidad en el horizonte de la guerra (Cuba 1868–1898).* San Juan, Puerto Rico: Editorial de la Universidad de Puerto Rico, 1999.

Mañach, Jorge. *Martí el apóstol.* (1933). Reprint ed. Madrid: Espasa Calpe, 1968.

——. *Martí, Apostle of Freedom.* Trans. Coley Taylor. New York: Devin-Adan Co., 1950.

Martí, Oscar R. "José Martí and the Heroic Image." In Belnap and Fernández. 317–38.

Martí, José. *Diario de campaña (De Cabo Haitiano a Dos Ríos).* Ed. Nuria Gregori. Separata de *Anuario* L/L No. 1. Havana: Instituto de Literatura y Lingüística de la Academia de Ciencias de Cuba, 1972.

——. *Diarios de campaña.* Ed. Mayra Beatriz Martínez and Froilán Escobar. La Habana: Casa Editora Abrio, 1996.

——. *Ismaelillo. Versos libres. Versos sencillos.* Edited by Ivan Schulman. Madrid: Cátedra, 1987.

——. *Obras completas.* Havana: Editorial de Ciencias Sociales, 1975.

——. *The Selected Writings of José Martí.* Translated and edited by Esther Allen. New York: Penguin Classics, 2002.

Martínez-Echazábal, Lourdes. " 'Martí and Race': A Re-evaluation." In *Re-reading Martí*. Ed. J. Rodríguez-Luis. 115–126.

Masso, José Luis. *Camino de Dos Ríos*. Miami: Echevarría Printing, 1966.

Mirabal, Nancy Raquel. " 'Más que negro': José Martí and the Politics of Unity." *José Martí in the United States. The Florida Experience*. Ed. Louis A. Pérez. Tempe, AZ: ASU Center for Latin Américan Studies, 1995. 57–69.

Mitchell, Charles E. *Individualism and its Discontents. Appropriations of Emerson, 1880–1950*. Amherst: University of Massachusetts Press, 1997.

Molloy, Sylvia. "His America, Our America: José Martí Reads Whitman." *Modern Language Quarterly* 57.2 (June 1996): 371–379.

Moon, Michael. *Disseminating Whitman. Revision and Corporeality in* Leaves of Grass. Cambridge, MA: Harvard University Press, 1991.

Mosse, George L. *Nationalism and Sexuality. Middle-Class Morality and Sexual Norms in Modern Europe*. Madison: The University of Wisconsin Press, 1985.

"Mrs. Pickett's Reception. Honored on the Battlefield of Gettysburg. Union and Confederate Veterans Comparing Notes on the Scene of their Memorable Struggle." *New York Times* July 5, 1887: 1.

"The Oak Ridge Riot. Twelve Negroes and One White Man Killed." *New York Times* July 5, 1887: 1.

Ober, Frederick. "Interesting Cuba." Pamphlet included in *Pamphlets on Cuba*, n.d. Butler Library. Columbia University.

O'Rell, Max [pseud. of Paul Blouët] and Allyn, Jack. *Jonathan and his Continent: Rambles through American society*. Translated by Madame Paul Blouët. New York: Cassell, 1889.

Ortiz, Fernando. *Martí y las razas*. Havana: Comisión Nacional Organizadora de los Actos y Ediciones del Centenario y del Monumento de Martí, 1953.

Oviedo, José Miguel. *La niña de Nueva York*. Mexico: Fondo de Cultura Económica, 1989.

Paz, Octavio. *Children of the Mire: Modern Poetry from Romanticism to the Avant-Garde*. Translated by Rachel Phillips. Cambridge, MA: Harvard University Press, 1974.

Pérez, Louis A. *Cuba: Between Reform and Revolution*. New York: Oxford University Press, 1988.

——, ed. *José Martí in the United States: The Florida Experience*. Tempe, AZ: ASU Center for Latin American Studies, 1995.

Pérez Firmat, Gustavo. *The Cuban Condition: Translation and Identity in Modern Cuban Literature*. Cambridge, UK: Cambridge University Press, 1989.

Pilat, Oliver. *Sodom by the Sea: An Affectionate History of Coney Island*. Garden City, N.Y.: Doubleday, Doran & Co., 1941.

"The Race Prejudice." *Sun* [New York] July 7, 1887: 2.

Rama, Angel. "La dialéctica de la Modernidad en José Martí." *Estudios martianos* (Collection of papers presented at a Martí symposium at the University of Puerto Rico, February 1971). San Juan, Puerto Rico: Editorial Universitaria, 1974.

Ramos, Julio. *Divergent Modernities. Culture and Politics in Nineteenth Century Latin America.* Trans. John D. Blanco. Durham, NC: Duke University Press, 2001.

———. *Paradojas de la letra.* Caracas: Ediciones eXcultura, 1996.

Raper, Arthur Franklin. *The Tragedy of Lynching.* Chapel Hill, University of North Carolina Press, 1933.

"Reunion at Gettysburg. Survivors of the Blue and the Gray Unite in a Camp Fire." *Sun* [New York] July 3, 1887:10.

Riis, Jacob A. *How the Other Half Lives.* 1890. New York: Penguin Books, 1997.

Ripoll, Carlos. *La vida íntima y secreta de José Martí.* New York: Editorial Dos Ríos, 1995.

Rodríguez-Luis, Julio, ed. *Re-reading José Martí (1853–1895). One Hundred Years later.* Albany, NY: State University of New York Press, 1991.

Rojas, Rafael. *José Martí: la invención de Cuba.* Madrid: Colibrí, 2000.

Roosevelt, Theodore. *The Rough Riders.* New York: Charles Scribner's Sons, 1911.

Rotker, Susana. *La invención de la crónica.* Buenos Aires: Ediciones Letra Buena, 1992.

Rowan, Andrew Summers, and Ramsey, Marathon Montrose. *The Island of Cuba: A descriptive and historical account of the "Great Antilla."* New York: Henry Holt & Co., 1897.

Santí, Enrico Mario. *"Ismaelillo,* Martí y el modernismo." *Escritura y tradición. Texto, crítica y poética en la literatura hispanoamericana.* Barcelona: Laia, 1988. 159–189.

———. "Jose Martí and the Cuban Revolution." *Cuban Studies/Estudios Cubanos* 16 (1986): 139–150.

———. "Thinking through Martí." In *Re-reading José Martí.* Ed. L. Rodríguez-Luis. 67–83.

Schulman, Ivan A. "Desde los Estados Unides: Martí y las minorías étnicas y culturales." *Los Ensayistas* 10–11 (March 1981). University of Georgia Press, 1981. 139–152.

———. "Void and renewal: José Martí's modernity." In Abel and Torrents, eds. 153–175.

Showalter, Elaine. *Sexual Anarchy: Gender and Culture at the Fin de Siècle.* New York: Penguin Books, 1990.

Sommer, Doris. *Foundational Fictions: The National Romances of Latin America.* Berkeley: University of California Press, 1991.

———. "José Martí, Author of Walt Whitman." In Belnap and Fernández. 77–90.

Toledo Sande, Luis. *Cesto de llamas: biografía de José Martí.* Havana: Editorial de Ciencias Sociales, 2000.

Veblen, Thorstein. *The Theory of the Leisure Class.* 1899; New York: The Modern Library, 1934.

Vera-León, Antonio. "A Garden of Forking Tongues: Bicultural Subjects and an Ethics of Circulating in and out of Ethnicities." *Apuntes posmodernos/ Postmodern Notes* 3.2 (Spring 1993): 10–19.

Vitier, Cintio. *Lo cubano en la poesía*. La Habana: Instituto del Libro, 1970.

Vitier, Cintio, and García Marruz, Fina. *Temas martianos*. Río Piedras, Puerto Rico: Ediciones Huracán, 1981.

"A War of Races. Six Louisiana Negroes Shot in a Battle with Whites, and Six Lynched." *Sun* [New York] July 5, 1887: 2.

Wells-Barnett, Ida B. *Southern Horrors and Other Writings: The Anti-lynching Campaign of Ida B. Wells, 1892–1900*. Edited and with an introduction by Jacqueline Jones Royster. Boston: Bedford Books, 1997.

West, Cornel. *The American Evasion of Philosophy: A Genealogy of Pragmatism*. Madison: University of Wisconsin Press, 1989.

Whitaker, Arthur P. *The Western Hemisphere Idea. Its Rise and Decline*. Ithaca, NY: Cornell University Press, 1954.

Williamson, Joel. *A Rage for Order. Black/White Relations in the American South since Reconstruction*. New York: Oxford University Press, 1986.

Wordsworth, William. *The Poetical Works of William Wordsworth*. Edited by Thomas Hutchinson. London: Oxford University Press, 1913.

II. MARTÍ IN ENGLISH

The America of José Martí. Selected Writings. Edited by Juan de Onís. New York: Noonday Press, 1953.

Inside the Monster. Writings on the United States and American Imperialism. Translated by Elinor Randall. With additional translations by Luis A. Baralt, Juan de Onís and Roslyn Held Foner. Edited, with an Introduction and notes, by Philip S. Foner. New York and London: Monthly Review Press, 1975.

José Martí Reader: Writings on the Americas. New York: Ocean Press, 1999. Edited by Deborah Shnookal and Mirta Muñiz. Introduction by Ivan A. Schulman. Melbourne, Australia: Ocean Press, 1999.

José Martí: Thoughts on Liberty, Government, Art and Morality: A Bilingual Anthology. Edited by Carlos Ripoll. New York: Las Américas, 1985.

Major Poems. A bilingual edition. Translation by Elinor Randall. Edited, with an introduction by Philip S. Foner. New York and London: Holmes & Meier Publishers, Inc., 1982.

Martí on the U.S.A. Selected and translated, with an introduction by Luis A. Baralt. Foreword by J. Cary Davis. Carbondale and Edwardsville: Southern Illinois University Press, 1966.

On Art and Literature: Critical Writings. Translated by Elinor Randall. With additional translations by Luis A. Baralt, Juan de Onís and Roslyn Held Foner. Edited, with an Introduction and notes, by Philip S. Foner. New York and London: Monthly Review Press, 1982.

On Education: Articles on Educational Theory and Pedagogy, and Writings for Children from The Age of Gold. Translated by Elinor Randall. Edited, with an Introduction and notes, by Philip S. Foner. New York: Monthly Review Press, 1979.

Our America: Writings on Latin America and the Struggle for Cuban Independence. Translated by Elinor Randall. With additional translations by Juan de Onís and Roslyn Held Foner. Edited, with an Introduction and notes by Philip S. Foner. New York and London: Monthly Review Press, 1977.

Political Parties and Elections in the United States. Edited, with an introduction and notes, by Philip S. Foner. Translated by Elinor Randall. Philadelphia: Temple University Press, 1989.

Selected Writings. Edited and translated by Esther Allen. Introduction by Roberto González Echevarría. New York: Penguin Books, 2002.

Versos sencillos/Simple Verses. Translated by Manuel A. Tellechea. Houston, Texas: Arte Público Press, 1997.